AL
SHARPTON

AL
SHARPTON

Hal Marcovitz

CHELSEA HOUSE PUBLISHERS
Philadelphia

Chelsea House Publishers

Editor in Chief	Sally Cheney
Director of Production	Kim Shinners
Production Manager	Pamela Loos
Art Director	Sara Davis

Staff for AL SHARPTON

Associate Art Director	Takeshi Takahashi
Layout	21st Century Publishing and Communications
Senior Editor	LeeAnne Gelletly
Production Editor	Diann Grasse

The Chelsea House World Wide Web address is
http://www.chelseahouse.com

First Printing

1 3 5 7 9 8 6 4 2

Library of Congress Cataloging-in-Publication Data

Marcovitz, Hal.
Al Sharpton / by Hal Marcovitz.
    p.   cm. — (Black Americans of achievement)
Includes bibliographical references and index.
Summary: The life and achievements of Al Sharpton, minister, civil rights
activist, and politician.
ISBN 0-7910-6295-3 (alk. paper) — ISBN 0-7910-6296-1 (pbk. : alk. paper)
1. Sharpton, Al—Juvenile literature. 2. African Americans—Biography—Juvenile
literature. 3. African American clergy—New York (State)—New York—Biography
—Juvenile literature. 4. Clergy—New York (State)—New York—Biography—
Juvenile literature. 5. Politicians—New York (State)—New York—Biography—
Juvenile literature. 6. African American politicians—New York (State)—New
York—Biography—Juvenile literature. 7. new York (N.Y.)—Biography—Juvenile
literature. [1. Sharpton, Al. 2. Clergy. 3. Politicians. 4. Civil rights workers.
5. African Americans—Biography.] I. Title. II. Series.
E185.97.S54 M37 2001
974.7'100496073'0092—dc21
[B]
                                                    2001042078

Frontispiece:
Al Sharpton Jr. makes a public statement for the media. An impassioned activist and minister, Sharpton seems always to be in front of either a TV camera or a pulpit.

CONTENTS

BLACK AMERICANS OF ACHIEVEMENT

HENRY AARON
baseball great

KAREEM ABDUL-JABBAR
basketball great

MUHAMMAD ALI
heavyweight champion

RICHARD ALLEN
religious leader and social activist

MAYA ANGELOU
author

LOUIS ARMSTRONG
musician

ARTHUR ASHE
tennis great

JOSEPHINE BAKER
entertainer

TYRA BANKS
model

BENJAMIN BANNEKER
scientist and mathematician

COUNT BASIE
bandleader and composer

ANGELA BASSETT
actress

ROMARE BEARDEN
artist

HALLE BERRY
actress

MARY MCLEOD BETHUNE
educator

GEORGE WASHINGTON
CARVER
botanist

JOHNNIE COCHRAN
lawyer

BILL COSBY
entertainer

MILES DAVIS
musician

FREDERICK DOUGLASS
abolitionist editor

CHARLES DREW
physician

PAUL LAURENCE DUNBAR
poet

DUKE ELLINGTON
bandleader and composer

RALPH ELLISON
author

JULIUS ERVING
basketball great

LOUIS FARRAKHAN
political activist

ELLA FITZGERALD
singer

ARETHA FRANKLIN
entertainer

MORGAN FREEMAN
actor

MARCUS GARVEY
black nationalist leader

JOSH GIBSON
baseball great

WHOOPI GOLDBERG
entertainer

DANNY GLOVER
actor

CUBA GOODING JR.
actor

ALEX HALEY
author

PRINCE HALL
social reformer

JIMI HENDRIX
musician

MATTHEW HENSON
explorer

GREGORY HINES
performer

BILLIE HOLIDAY
singer

LENA HORNE
entertainer

WHITNEY HOUSTON
singer and actress

LANGSTON HUGHES
poet

JANET JACKSON
musician

JESSE JACKSON
civil-rights leader and politician

MICHAEL JACKSON
entertainer

SAMUEL L. JACKSON
actor

T. D. JAKES
religious leader

JACK JOHNSON
heavyweight champion

MAE JEMISON
astronaut

MAGIC JOHNSON
basketball great

SCOTT JOPLIN
composer

BARBARA JORDAN
politician

MICHAEL JORDAN
basketball great

CORETTA SCOTT KING
civil-rights leader

MARTIN LUTHER KING, JR.
civil-rights leader

LEWIS LATIMER
scientist

SPIKE LEE
filmmaker

CARL LEWIS
champion athlete

RONALD MCNAIR
astronaut

MALCOLM X
militant black leader

BOB MARLEY
musician

THURGOOD MARSHALL
Supreme Court justice

TERRY MCMILLAN
author

TONI MORRISON
author

ELIJAH MUHAMMAD
religious leader

EDDIE MURPHY
entertainer

JESSE OWENS
champion athlete

SATCHEL PAIGE
baseball great

CHARLIE PARKER
musician

ROSA PARKS
civil-rights leader

COLIN POWELL
military leader

QUEEN LATIFAH
entertainer

DELLA REESE
entertainer

PAUL ROBESON
singer and actor

JACKIE ROBINSON
baseball great

CHRIS ROCK
comedian and actor

DIANA ROSS
entertainer

AL SHARPTON
minister and activist

WILL SMITH
actor

WESLEY SNIPES
actor

CLARENCE THOMAS
Supreme Court justice

SOJOURNER TRUTH
antislavery activist

HARRIET TUBMAN
antislavery activist

NAT TURNER
slave revolt leader

TINA TURNER
entertainer

ALICE WALKER
author

MADAM C. J. WALKER
entrepreneur

BOOKER T. WASHINGTON
educator

DENZEL WASHINGTON
actor

J. C. WATTS
politician

VANESSA WILLIAMS
singer and actress

VENUS WILLIAMS
tennis star

OPRAH WINFREY
entertainer

TIGER WOODS
golf star

ON ACHIEVEMENT

—◆—

Coretta Scott King

Before you begin this book, I hope you will ask yourself what the word *excellence* means to you. I think it's a question we should all ask, and keep asking as we grow older and change. Because the truest answer to it should never change. When you think of excellence, perhaps you think of success at work; or of becoming wealthy; or meeting the right person, getting married, and having a good family life.

Those goals are worth striving for, but there is a better way to look at excellence. As Martin Luther King Jr. said in one of his last sermons, "I want you to be first in love. I want you to be first in moral excellence. I want you to be first in generosity. If you want to be important, wonderful. If you want to be great, wonderful. But recognize that he who is greatest among you shall be your servant."

My husband knew that the true meaning of achievement is service. When I met him, in 1952, he was already ordained as a Baptist minister and was working toward a doctoral degree at Boston University. I was studying at the New England Conservatory and dreamed of accomplishments in music. We married a year later, and after I graduated the following year we moved to Montgomery, Alabama. We didn't know it then, but our notions of achievement were about to undergo a dramatic change.

You may have read or heard about what happened next. What began with the boycott of a local bus line grew into a national crusade, and by the time he was assassinated in 1968 my husband had fashioned a black movement powerful enough to shatter forever the practice of racial segregation. What you may not have read about is where he learned to resist injustice without compromising his religious beliefs.

He adopted a strategy of nonviolence from a man of a different race, who lived in a different country and even practiced a different religion. The man was Mahatma Gandhi, the great leader of India, who devoted his life to serving humanity in the spirit of love and nonviolence. It was in these principles that Martin discovered his method for social reform. More than anything else, those two principles were the key to his achievements.

These books are about African Americans who served society through the excellence of their achievements. They form part of the rich history of black men and women in America—a history of stunning accomplishments in every field of human endeavor, from literature and art to science, industry, education, diplomacy, athletics, jurisprudence, even polar exploration.

Not all of the people in this history had the same ideals, but I think you will find that all of them had something in common. Like Martin Luther King Jr., they all decided to become "drum majors" and serve humanity. In that principle—whether it was expressed in books, inventions, or song—they found a goal and a guide outside themselves that showed them a way to serve others instead of living only for themselves.

Reading the stories of these courageous men and women not only helps us discover the principles that we will use to guide our own lives; it also teaches us about our black heritage and about America itself. It is crucial for us to know the heroes and heroines of our history and to realize that the price we paid in our struggle for equality in America was dear. But we must also understand that we have gotten as far as we have partly because America's democratic system and ideals made it possible.

We are still struggling with racism and prejudice. But the great men and women in this series are a tribute to the spirit of the country in which they have flourished. And that makes their stories special and worth knowing.

1

BENSONHURST

❧

IT WAS A cold, windswept day on the streets of Bensonhurst as the car carrying the Reverend Al Sharpton arrived at Public School 205 on 20th Avenue. All day, the sun had been unable to pierce the heavy gray clouds that hung over the city. But on the streets below, tempers were on fire. It was just before 1 P.M. on January 12, 1991, and Bensonhurst was ready to explode.

Some 17 months before, a young black man named Yusuf Hawkins had been killed in front of P.S. 205 as he fled a gang of 30 white youths. Hawkins had ventured into the Brooklyn, New York City, neighborhood in search of a car he knew to be for sale, but a false rumor had circulated among approximately 30 angry young men on the predominantly white Bensonhurst streets—a report that blacks were coming to their neighborhood to stir up trouble. Sadly, by the time the 17-year-old Hawkins innocently stepped onto 20th Avenue, the gang's emotions had been stirred up to a blind hatred for blacks, and Hawkins became the victim of its rage. The violent murder had shocked and outraged the black community in New York.

The Brooklyn district attorney's office won convictions against many of Hawkins's attackers, but to Sharpton and other black leaders, the convictions

Sharpton makes a public statement after the August 1989 shooting of Yusuf Hawkins. Sharpton's reaction to the court trial of Hawkins' attackers, as well as to the attack on his life 16 months later, would ultimately strengthen his reputation as a civil rights activist.

An angry Sharpton storms out of a state supreme court building, clasping the hand of Diane Hawkins, mother of the slain Yusuf Hawkins. The activist Sharpton accused the court of being too lenient on Hawkins' offenders.

and sentences handed down to the men who killed Yusuf Hawkins were not serious enough. Just a few days before Sharpton arrived back at P.S. 205, two of the attackers—John Vento and Joseph Serrano—had been convicted of minor charges in connection with the Hawkins case. Eventually only one of Hawkins's 30 attackers, Joseph Fama, would be convicted of murder.

Sharpton believed that the Vento and Serrano verdicts were insults to the black community, and he decided to stage a march through the streets of Bensonhurst to demonstrate the community's disgust over the verdicts. He chose the school yard of P.S. 205 as the starting-off point for the march.

In his autobiography, *Go and Tell Pharaoh*, Sharpton wrote: "The most horrible thing about the way these cases were swept under the rug every time a black person was killed is that it became normal. It became the expected thing. It devalued everyone's life. . . . So the more value I put on a kid's life, enough to stop the city for a day, the more the killer has to think, maybe this is wrong."

Sharpton, who grew up on the tough inner-city streets of Crown Heights in Brooklyn, was a veteran political organizer who had been staging demonstrations against injustice since the age of 10. With just a few phone calls, Sharpton could set in motion a well-organized network capable of drawing out crowds of his supporters for protest marches, sit-ins, boycotts, and other acts of nonviolent civil disobedience. By 1991, he was one of New York's most familiar black leaders: a large, portly man with wavy hair and a fondness for jogging suits. Indeed, his fiery oratorical skills had been honed since the age of four when he delivered his first church sermon.

Sharpton staged the Bensonhurst protest march on January 12, 1991, three days before Martin Luther King Jr. Day. Dr. King was a dynamic figure in the civil rights movement who was shot to death in 1968 on the balcony of a motel in Memphis, Tennessee. King had been one of young Al Sharpton's heroes and had served as Sharpton's model of civil disobedience—a philosophy that affirms nonviolent resistance as the most effective form of social protest.

Some 500 people responded to Sharpton's call for action that day and were waiting through the blustery January weather in the P.S. 205 school yard. But not everyone in the crowd showed up to hear the speeches and march in protest to the Vento and Serrano verdicts. One member of the crowd with a different plan was Michael Riccardi, a 28-year-old white man who lived in Bensonhurst, not far from P.S. 205.

Riccardi had led a troubled youth—he had been arrested numerous times on a variety of charges. He was a heavy drinker. In fact, he was drunk the morning of January 12 when he heard that Al Sharpton would be speaking at a rally later that day at P.S. 205.

Riccardi lived in a tiny basement apartment on 73rd Street. He barely eked out a living as a street vendor, selling trinkets and souvenirs to tourists. On the morning of January 12 Michael Riccardi was drunk and angry. He decided to go to Al Sharpton's protest march. Before leaving his apartment, Riccardi tucked a five-inch kitchen knife under his jacket.

When Sharpton's car arrived at P.S. 205, he discovered that the police had surrounded the school yard with some 100 officers, although with the atmosphere so tense it wasn't clear to him whether the police were there to protect the marchers or intimidate them. The police set up what is known as a "frozen area." Their intention was to separate the protesters from angry members of the crowd who had showed up to heckle the protesters and shout insults at them as they made their way through the Bensonhurst streets. Clearly, though, the frozen area had a few holes. Dozens of people had slipped through the blue wall surrounding the school yard.

The car carrying Sharpton parked in the school yard. Sharpton remained in the vehicle for several

minutes, waiting for his assistants to give him the signal that the march was organized and ready to begin. Waiting in the car with Sharpton was Moses Stewart, Yusuf Hawkins's father.

"Finally, my assistant, Carl Redding, walked over and said it was time, they were ready for me, and I got out of the car and walked toward the front of the line," Sharpton said. "We were still, remember, inside the playground, which was supposed to be a secure area, and I turned my head to say something to Carl."

"Sharpton!" cried a voice in the throng of people. It was Michael Riccardi—he had made his way to the front of the crowd and lunged forward as he yelled Sharpton's name. Sharpton turned his head to see who had shouted. Suddenly, he felt

Sharpton leads supporters of Yusuf Hawkins in a march protesting what many believed to be an unjust verdict. Joseph Fama would be the only defendant convicted of murder; the rest were either convicted of assault or received no sentence at all.

what he thought was a punch in the chest. "I saw this face, a white male, flash past me," Sharpton recalled later. "He had this contorted look of hatred on his face, a real look of hate, I'll never forget that, and before I could get a clear look at him I looked down and saw a knife sticking out of my chest. I thought, 'Oh my God, he stabbed me.'"

Sharpton grabbed the handle of the knife and pulled it out. That's when the pain hit him. He fell to his knees and saw his hands covered in blood.

Riccardi dashed away as soon as he thrust the knife into Sharpton's chest, but he didn't get far. Sharpton's assistant, Carl Redding, is a former professional football player and quickly tackled the assailant. Moses Stewart and Henry Johnson, another of Sharpton's assistants, dove into the melee and attempted to hold Riccardi for the police, but when the officers managed to push their way through the crowd and saw three black men wrestling with one white man, they responded by beating Redding, Stewart, and Johnson. Finally, somebody convinced the officers that Riccardi was the assailant, and the police took him into custody.

Amidst the confusion, nobody thought to call an ambulance for Sharpton. After Riccardi was apprehended, some supporters helped Sharpton to a nearby car, and he was driven to Coney Island Hospital. The ride took 10 minutes. Doctors made X rays of the wound and determined that the knife had sunk three inches into Sharpton's chest and his lungs were filling with blood. The doctors acted quickly to drain the lungs and sew up the wound. Certainly, the wound had been serious but Sharpton was lucky—the knife had narrowly missed his heart and major arteries.

In the hospital's recovery room, many of the city's political leaders gathered around Sharpton's bedside. One of those leaders was David N. Dinkins,

the mayor of New York and a longtime associate of Sharpton.

As Sharpton faded in and out of consciousness from the anesthesia, he said these words: "Tell Jesse to call me." What he meant was he wanted to speak with the Reverend Jesse Jackson, Sharpton's mentor for years who, after the death of Martin Luther King, had become the nation's most influential civil rights leader.

Later that night, after Sharpton emerged from the stupor of the anesthesia, he did speak on the phone with Jackson, who was in Washington, D.C. "There's too much racism in this country and if I survive I hope I'm going to be even more serious

After the 1991 stabbing at the Bensonhurt rally, a recovering Sharpton receives a visit from longtime mentor and friend, the Reverend Jesse Jackson. Although the attack was a terrifying ordeal, Sharpton believes it made him a humbler person.

now in the true King tradition of opposing it," Sharpton said.

Jackson was moved by their conversation. He rushed up to New York and by 7 A.M. the next morning was in Sharpton's hospital room.

Jackson had concluded that with Sharpton's organizational abilities and his gift for stirring up emotions in people's hearts, the firebrand minister could become one of the nation's great spokesmen for civil rights, but that at this point his energies lacked direction. After Sharpton left the hospital, Jackson arranged for him to meet with Cornel West, a professor of religion at Princeton University, in New Jersey. The black community reveres West as somebody who speaks clearly on the true meaning of social justice.

West urged Sharpton "to work toward building bridges between whites and blacks." West's words hit Sharpton like a bolt of lightning. "I realized I was a *Christian* activist, out of the tradition of Adam Clayton Powell, Martin Luther King, and Jesse Jackson, a minister. . . . I come out of Martin's house," Sharpton said.

Later, West told a reporter that Sharpton "has the courage and the talent. Does he have the perseverance and the humility?"

Sharpton realized after he recovered that the stabbing, followed by his conversation with Jackson, represented a turning point in his life and in his work as a black leader. No longer would Sharpton be simply a street activist—he would now work on a higher plane, to influence the hearts and minds of the leaders in the political arena.

Al Sharpton would have the opportunity to demonstrate his new philosophy in dealing with his attacker, Michael Riccardi. Could he forgive the man who tried to murder him?

After the incident at P.S. 205, Riccardi had been hustled away by police, who charged him

Sharpton speaks with Cornel West, a renowned intellectual and expert on race issues. In 1991, Jesse Jackson arranged a meeting, where West reminded Sharpton that he comes from a great tradition of activist ministers.

with a number of crimes, the most serious of which was attempted murder. He came to trial in February 1992.

During the trial, Riccardi admitted to drinking heavily the morning of January 12, 1991. Prosecutors alleged that Riccardi had deliberately stalked Sharpton that day. Assistant District Attorney Edward Boyar told jurors that the protest march had been staged during a particularly volatile time in New York's race relations, and that the attack on Sharpton could have provoked "a highly explosive and highly charged situation that could have resulted in even more violence."

After a two-week trial, Riccardi was convicted by the jury on February 24 of assault and possession of a weapon, but acquitted of the most serious charge—attempted murder. The jury also returned a verdict of not guilty to the charges that the attack on Sharpton had been racially motivated. Sentencing was set for March 16.

While Michael Riccardi sat in jail, awaiting sentencing, he received a visit by a most unexpected guest: Al Sharpton.

Sharpton emerged from the meeting convinced that Riccardi was not a racist, and that the man had been led astray by the media's portrayal of Al Sharpton as a brash advocate for black power. When court convened on March 16, Sharpton rose in his seat and addressed Judge Francis X. Egitto, asking for leniency for Riccardi, calling him "a victim of racial tensions created by media hype."

Egitto still aimed to hand down a tough sentence. Riccardi was sent to prison for a term of 5 to 15 years. His attorney, Joyce David, said Riccardi realizes now that he was wrong, and that he waits anxiously for the day when he can be released from jail to begin a new life. "He was just a kid who did something stupid," she said.

For Sharpton, though, the attack served to begin changing him from the hard-charging activist—considered by some a fiery rabble-rouser—to a more thoughtful human being, somebody who could find it in his heart to forgive a man who had tried to kill him.

"You know, everybody grows," Sharpton said. "And I think everybody has certain turning points. For some, it's graduation from school, for others it's when a child is born. The stabbing, for me, was a turning point. I had been moving that way, anyway; I think the stabbing just consolidated it. It's time to go to the next step."

Reflecting on Cornel West's advice and his new approach as activist, Sharpton also said: "Cornel felt I was taking cheap shots. It hit me—you can really die for this stuff, and if you are going to die, at least be well defined in what you were doing and what made it worthwhile."

2

THE BOY PREACHER

A LFRED CHARLES SHARPTON Jr. was born on October 3, 1954, into a home unlike most others in the black community at that time. His father, Alfred Sharpton Sr., was a prosperous carpenter. Soon, he would provide his family a comfortable home in a middle-class neighborhood in Queens, a borough of New York City.

In the 1950s, few blacks owned their own homes or businesses. In the southern states, many blacks found themselves existing below the poverty line as they eked out livings as farm laborers or domestics in the homes of whites. A black home in the South during that time was typically a tiny shack with no indoor plumbing and electricity; indeed, blacks experienced few of the new 1950s-style luxuries, such as electric ranges, refrigerators, television sets, or washers and dryers, that their white employers enjoyed.

And so many blacks fled north seeking a better life, although conditions were rarely better in the states above the Mason-Dixon Line. In the North, most black families lived in crowded apartments in big cities, which were just beginning to see the urban decay that would nearly ruin downtown districts in the years following World War II. During this time white investment flowed out of the cities and into the surrounding suburbs that seemed to spring up virtually overnight.

A young Sharpton, age seven, preaches from a pulpit at his home church. By this point, Sharpton had already been preaching for three years. In 1964, Bishop Washington ordained Sharpton, only 10 years old, as a Pentecostal minister.

Among the blacks who fled north in search of new opportunities were Alfred Sharpton Sr. and Ada Richards Glasgow. The two would meet in Brooklyn.

Ada was born in Dothan, Alabama, a small town located on the Alabama-Florida border. Her father died shortly after she was born. Ada married at an early age, but her marriage to John Glasgow didn't work out, and she divorced him and moved north to Brooklyn with her two children, Thomas and Ernestine

Soon after Ada's arrival in Brooklyn, she met Al Sharpton, who had moved north from Vero Beach, Florida. Sharpton, who was one of 17 children, had also been previously married and divorced. By the time they were married, Al was already a busy carpenter who would go on to own assorted businesses, real estate, and his own contracting company.

The Sharpton's first child, Cheryl, was born in 1951. Al Jr. followed three years later. The family settled first in a small home in Brooklyn, but because Al Sr. was doing so well the Sharptons decided to buy a large, comfortable home in the Hollis neighborhood of Queens.

"[Our home] had a finished basement, a raised lawn all the way around the corner of the house, and a small apartment upstairs, which we rented out," Sharpton remembered. "The address was 100-50 199th Street, Hollis, Queens. Black middle class. I think another reason we moved was that my parents wanted me and my sister to go to school in Queens instead of Brooklyn. At one point my father was doing so well he bought two Cadillacs every year, one for my mother, one for him."

Among the Sharptons' neighbors were the singers Brooke Benton and James Brown, and jazz band leader Count Basie,

After moving to Queens, Ada and Al Sharpton continued to return every Sunday to Brooklyn, where they belonged to the Washington Temple Church of God in Christ, a Pentecostal church. The primary

belief of the Pentecostal Church is that Jesus Christ will return to the earth during a period that is referred to as the "Second Coming." Many followers of the Pentecostal Church also believe God has the power to heal illnesses and injuries and that he speaks through the mouths of his people in languages unheard before. This is known as "speaking in tongues." Pentecostals are also known for their lively church services, which include inspirational rhetoric from the pulpit and wild, uncontrolled outbursts from members of the congregation. The church is predominantly African-American and, compared to most other Protestant sects, is relatively young, having been founded in 1906 by William J. Seymour.

At Washington Temple, the Sharptons were very moved by the rousing sermons of its minister, Bishop Frederick Douglass Washington. "Bishop Washington was a truly great man, one of the kind of leaders of the self-contained black community that we rarely see

The Washington Temple in Brooklyn, New York. Through his loyal participation in church activities and events, Sharpton met many influential activist leaders like Adam Clayton Powell Jr. and Martin Luther King Jr.

anymore," Sharpton later recalled. "He was a phenomenal preacher in the southern 'whooping' tradition, that singsong way of preaching that can just transport a congregation when it's done correctly. But at the same time, he was an intellectual, he'd read and studied, he'd thought about things."

Al and his sister Cheryl Sharpton accompanied their parents to church every Sunday. Bishop Washington's sermons made such a deep impression on Al that one day, while attending a youth group meeting at the church, the little boy told an adult leader of the group that he wanted to preach a sermon. On July 9, 1959, four-year-old Al Sharpton Jr., wearing a gold robe that his mother had made for him, stood on a box before the congregation of about 800 members and preached the sermon "Let Not Your Heart Be Troubled" at the Washington Temple in Brooklyn.

"I just felt the compulsion, the calling," said Sharpton. "And fortunately, we had a pastor who gave me the opportunity. I just went full-steam ahead, thanks to Bishop Washington."

Congregants were so stirred by the boy's performance that they asked Bishop Washington to permit Al to deliver more sermons. Washington soon appointed Sharpton junior pastor at the church, and the boy found himself leading many of the sermons at Washington Temple. Later, other churches around the city learned of the young boy's oratorical skills, and they asked him to preach as well. Black churches throughout New York City were anxious to hear sermons delivered by the "Boy Preacher."

Sharpton recalled that his job as junior pastor made for a unique relationship with his playmates: "I'd play stickball on Friday night and on Sunday their parents were going to hear me preach," he said.

When Sharpton turned seven, his family took a car trip south to visit relatives. It was on this trip that the cold reality of prejudice hit Sharpton squarely in the face. South of the Mason-Dixon Line, Sharpton

became aware of the "Whites Only" signs posted on the windows of restaurants, on signs in front of motels, and on the doors to restrooms. And those restaurants that did permit blacks to enter usually had an area of the dining room set aside specifically for African Americans. It was on this trip in the South that Al Sharpton Sr. told his son a story about the boy's grandfather, Coleman Sharpton. A group of whites had beaten him up at his home in Florida because he had refused to step off the curb and move out of their way.

A policeman places a segregation sign in front of a railroad station. When he was seven, Sharpton and his family took a trip through the South, where he got a first-hand lesson on segregation.

It was the early 1960s and the nation's civil rights movement in the United States was gaining momentum. In 1963, Al Sharpton Sr. went to Washington to participate in a march on the nation's capital led by Martin Luther King Jr., the head of an influential civil rights organization named the Southern Christian Leadership Conference.

Meanwhile, the Boy Preacher was hard at work at Washington Temple, honing his speaking skills and becoming involved in the church's activities in the community. Soon after the 1963 Washington march that Al Sr. attended, Martin Luther King Jr. went on a tour of the nation's black churches to raise the consciousness of black people about their rights. One of his stops was the Washington Temple in Brooklyn, where Bishop Washington introduced the great civil rights leader to the church's junior pastor.

Still just nine years old, the Boy Preacher had started asking questions about why blacks didn't seem to have the same rights as whites. Sharpton had already begun to observe the racism that inspired King and others to action. At home, for example, the Sharpton family would gather around the TV set on Sunday nights to watch the *Ed Sullivan Show*— the enormously popular variety show produced in New York that featured performances by the top music and comedy stars of the 1950s and 1960s. As Al Sharpton Jr. watched the Sullivan show, he wondered why he only occasionally saw black performers. Indeed, a star such as Nat King Cole, who was by far the most successful black entertainer of his day, was a guest only a handful of times on the show.

Sharpton later reflected on the show's muted racism: "Ed Sullivan was the epitome of American television at that time," Sharpton said. "And he was based in New York, so I think the exclusionary lineup of Ed Sullivan also reflected what was acceptable in chic New York circles. We're not talking about Ed

Sullivan broadcasting out of the South—he was right there on Broadway in New York, and it was acceptable that blacks were excluded from the show."

In 1964, Al Sharpton Jr. would face a difficult trial that may have ultimately turned him toward social activism. When he was 10 years old, Al and Ada Sharpton divorced. Al's father refused to help his family financially, and Ada was forced to leave the home in Queens and find a small apartment in a government housing project on the tough streets of Crown Heights, Brooklyn. There, Al and Cheryl Sharpton would spend the remainder of their childhoods.

"Our family's income went through the floor," Sharpton said. "It was very traumatic. . . . You go from a two-car garage, a 10-room house in Queens with a basement, to a housing project. I had never, until I was 10 years old, lived in a house my parents didn't own. I'd never been in a community where the garbage wasn't picked up on time, where the police didn't come if you called. And now I was in a housing project where people were stacked up on top of one another. And I knew that there was a better life than this. And that was probably what made me start seeking, to ask: How do you make things fair? Because I knew this was unfair, better than my playmates, because they knew of no other life."

After Al Sharpton Sr. left the family, Ada Sharpton was forced to go on welfare, the government's program to provide financial assistance to people in need.

Meanwhile, her son continued to preach at Washington Temple. When he was 10, Bishop Washington took the junior pastor with him on a tour of the Caribbean islands, including Barbados, Trinidad, Puerto Rico, Haiti and Jamaica. In Kingston, Jamaica, Sharpton was introduced to Amy Jacques Garvey, the widow of Marcus Garvey, founder of the Universal Negro Improvement Association, which had urged black people to be proud of their heritage and return to their ancestral homelands in Africa. Amy Jacques

African-American children partake in a sit-in at a luncheonette. As leader of the National Youth Movement, Sharpton would maintain the tradition of sit-ins and other forms of civil disobedience to effect social change.

Garvey and Al Sharpton met and talked for several hours about the work of her late husband, and in the years to follow they would carry on a correspondence by mail.

Back in New York, the Boy Preacher was asked to deliver a sermon before a show given by the gospel singer Mahalia Jackson attended by some 5,000 people at the New York World's Fair in 1964. Jackson was so impressed with Sharpton that she took him on tour with her across the country. When Sharpton returned from the tour, he managed to find time for his studies, rising at 5 A.M. each morning to take the elevated train to Public School 134 in Queens. Even though he was now living in Brooklyn, Sharpton had wanted to continue going to school in his old neighborhood.

And he continued to see to his duties as junior pastor at Washington Temple. Shortly after returning from the Caribbean, Bishop Washington ordained Sharpton a minister in the Pentecostal faith, meaning the Boy Preacher was now the Reverend Al Sharpton.

One Sunday morning, the Sharptons attended religious services at the Abyssinian Baptist Church in Harlem, where the Reverend Adam Clayton Powell Jr. preached. Powell, who was also a congressman, was the most influential black political figure of his day not only in New York City, but in the United States as well. First elected to Congress in 1944, by the mid-1960s Powell was chairman of the House Education and Labor Committee. As the powerful head of the committee, Powell consistently used a legislative clause called the "Powell Amendment," which when enacted would deny federal funding to any education or food program that did not give equal treatment to blacks.

Sharpton had a great respect for Powell's legacy: "I've always thought that Adam, because he represented to blacks the assumption of real power—you have to remember that for a long time he was the only black congressman—affected the body politic in a way that no other black leader did. He threatened the domestic picture of this country. I think that's why the media never really understood him, other than their predigested version of him as a troublemaker. The establishment didn't want blacks to emulate that independence, that self-assurance, that arrogance."

The Boy Preacher became a devoted follower of Adam Clayton Powell Jr., staying near Powell whenever the congressman returned to his Harlem district, running errands for him, helping to organize Powell's neighborhood programs, listening to his sermons at the Abyssinian church.

By now, Sharpton was 12 years old and attending junior high school in the Brooklyn neighborhood of

Flatbush. He became a dedicated reader, devouring books about his two heroes, Adam Clayton Powell Jr. and Marcus Garvey, as well as great thinkers and philosophers like Martin Luther King Jr. and Mohandas Gandhi, the great Hindu leader in India. King and Gandhi both wrote that equality could be won through the use of nonviolent civil disobedience.

Other authors who influenced Sharpton were Arnold Joseph Toynbee of Great Britain, who argued that many civilizations crumbled because they failed to adapt to moral and social changes, and Paul Johannes Tillich, an Evangelical Lutheran minister and philosopher born in Germany, who stated that belief in God still has relevancy in a society undergoing scientific and technological advancement.

When he wasn't locked in his room reading, Sharpton was out on the streets supporting his mentor Adam Clayton Powell Jr. In 1966, Powell found himself in legal as well as political trouble. He had been accused of siphoning off federal money earmarked for his staff's payroll. Soon, his fellow members of the House voted that Powell be expelled from Congress. Back in New York, many of Powell's supporters organized petition drives and other local efforts to bolster the veteran congressman's standing. Sharpton formed the "Youth Committee for Powell," which circulated petitions in black neighborhoods and churches demanding the congressman be reinstated to his seat. This issue provided Al Sharpton with his first experience as a political activist. The petitions he helped gather were sent to House Speaker John McCormack, and in 1967, in a special election to fill the vacant seat, Adam Clayton Powell Jr. was sent back to Washington by an overwhelming majority.

During one event in the campaign, Powell took Sharpton aside and gave him some important advice. He told the young activist: "There will come a time in life when you grow to be a great man, Alfred. The key to greatness is to do things in your generation

that seem unusual, but are really on time. And once you do that, then you can remove yourself from the scene. You don't have to push it until they kill you. You have to know when to hit it and when to quit it."

However, Adam Clayton Powell Jr. would not be on the scene much longer. Even though he had won his seat back in Congress, he was no longer the powerful political leader who ruled over the streets of his Harlem district. In 1969, Powell learned he had cancer. A year later, he was opposed for reelection by State Assemblyman Charles Rangel, who eked out a narrow victory over Powell. On April 4, 1972, Adam Clayton Powell Jr. died in Miami, Florida.

One activist who had a greater influence on Sharpton than any other was Adam Clayton Powell Jr., a minister and U.S. representative. Today, Sharpton still emulates Powell in his ability to bring about social change, as well as in his self-assurance and impassioned public speaking style.

Four years before Powell's death, Sharpton would lose another of his heroes: Martin Luther King Jr. He had gone to Memphis to support garbage collectors who were on strike in the city. On the afternoon of April 4, 1968, King stepped onto the balcony of the Lorraine Motel to head off to dinner when he was struck by a bullet fired by James Earl Ray. King was just 39 years old.

Sharpton clearly remembers the tragedy: "We were watching television that Thursday night when it came across the screen that he had been shot in Memphis. My mother started crying. I didn't understand why she was so upset, crying like he was a member of our family. I'd met Dr. King and admired him, but I didn't feel the personal connection. I asked my mother why she was taking it so hard, and she said that I would have to grow up in Alabama, have to spend my life going to the back of the bus, have had to travel miles holding my water when I needed a restroom while passing facilities I was forbidden to use, if I wanted to understand the meaning and importance of Martin Luther King. That has always stayed with me."

That fall, Al Sharpton entered Tilden High School in Brooklyn. On the streets, he saw many of his classmates turn to crime, drugs, and prostitution. His mother's purse was stolen by a black youth who snatched the handbag and ran. Sharpton could see the threat against blacks was coming not only from white society, which continued to deny blacks their civil rights, but also from other blacks, who were ready to commit violence against one another. One particular black leader, Reverend Jesse Jackson, counseled many young blacks to stay out of trouble and off drugs. Reverend Jackson was one of the men who was on that balcony in Memphis with King in April 1968.

In 1969, Jackson was heading Operation Breadbasket, a program started by King to organize boycotts of major American corporations that refused to open

their employment ranks to blacks. After Breadbasket targeted them with boycotts, companies such as Canada Dry, Wonder Bread, Sealtest, and Macy's Department Stores agreed to recruit more black workers.

Sharpton was active in the New York chapter of Breadbasket, and he soon met the local director of the program, the Reverend William C. Jones. Jones took the 14-year-old boy under his wing, buying books for Sharpton, taking him along as he made his rounds to Breadbasket functions, and introducing him to civil rights leaders who stopped off in New York. It was during one such visit that Sharpton met Jesse Jackson, one of the leaders on that New York visit. Jackson was so impressed with Sharpton that he appointed him youth director of Breadbasket.

"When I look back upon the men I was able to get to know when I was young," Sharpton said, "it astounds me whom I had access to and how good they were to me. In Bishop Washington, Adam Clayton

Dr. Reverend Martin Luther King Jr., flanked by the Reverend Jesse Jackson (left) and Ralph Abernathy (right), on the day before he was assassinated in 1968. As father of the nonviolent movement in the 1960s, King had an undeniable influence on Sharpton and other activists.

Powell and Jesse Jackson I could watch some of the greatest black leaders of our time very closely and learn from them."

As youth director of Breadbasket, Sharpton recruited 500 young people who could be regularly called on to attend rallies in New York City, where Breadbasket had targeted 23 companies for boycott. As an organizer of Breadbasket rallies, Sharpton employed some of the tactics he had learned from the writings of King and Gandhi—sit-ins, marches, speeches, blockades, and other forms of civil disobedience. Oftentimes, the police would make arrests at the demonstrations but because Sharpton was still a teenager, they never bothered to take him into custody, thinking that he posed no real threat.

Meanwhile, Sharpton was every bit the organizer at Tilden High School. He became president of the school's African-American Club and associate editor of the student newspaper, "The Gadfly." He was elected vice president of the debate team and head of the Martin Luther King Jr. Memorial Committee, which raised money for a portrait of the slain civil rights leader displayed in the school.

Sharpton spent his last year as youth director of Breadbasket in 1971. By then, a rift had formed in the Southern Christian Leadership Conference, with factions forming behind the Reverend Ralph Abernathy, who took over the SCLC following the assassination of King, and Jesse Jackson, who developed his own following among the younger members of the organization. In 1971, Jackson quit the SCLC amid charges that he had siphoned off money from an SCLC project known as Black Expo. The charges proved to be ungrounded. As for Jackson, he formed his own organization, People United to Save Humanity, or PUSH (later changed to People United to Serve Humanity). (In the 1980s he would also form another organization, the Rainbow Coalition, as the backbone of his campaigns for U. S. presidency in 1984 and 1988.)

When Jackson left the SCLC, Sharpton found himself caught in the middle. Reverend Jones elected to stay with organization, but Sharpton had become a devoted follower of Jesse Jackson. Still, he couldn't bring himself to break totally away from Reverend Jones; instead, Sharpton resolved to start up his own group—the National Youth Movement. He raised money from business leaders he met through his work in Breadbasket. Every activist group needs a lawyer, and Sharpton found one in an energetic black attorney from New York City named David Dinkins, who in later years would become mayor of New York

As leader of the National Youth Movement, Sharpton organized a Minority Youth Day in Brooklyn, attended the National Black Political Convention in Gary, Indiana, and helped draft the "Black Agenda" for political activism by minorities. Back home, he helped stage a Kwanzaa ceremony, becoming one of the first leaders to recognize the holiday designed to celebrate the African heritage of black people. His activities gained the notice of the press—The *New York Times* and *New York Daily News* ran profiles of the young black activist.

With Adam Clayton Powell out of Congress, Sharpton searched for a new political leader to help. He didn't have to search far. In 1972, New York's black congresswoman, Shirley Chisholm, took the bold move of running for the Democratic Party's nomination for president. Chisholm approached Sharpton and asked for his help in her campaign.

Sharpton immediately signed on and threw himself into the Chisholm campaign. But he did have to briefly take time off from helping to organize the national campaign for one important event in his life.

Al Sharpton had to graduate from high school.

3

THE GODFATHER

❦

IN MAY 1954, just a few months before Al Sharpton was born, the U.S. Supreme Court handed down a decision in a case known as *Brown v. Board of Education*. The case had been brought by the parents of Linda Brown, an eight-year-old black girl in Topeka, Kansas, who argued that the education their daughter was receiving at an all-black, segregated school was far inferior to the education white students in Topeka could expect at their schools.

Years before, in 1896, the Supreme Court ruled in the *Plessy v. Ferguson* case that railroad cars could be segregated as long as they were "separate but equal." Since then, school administrators in many states had applied that rationale to schools. Elsewhere, blacks were segregated in restrooms, restaurants, theaters, and other public places. But in *Brown v. Board of Education*, the Supreme Court struck down its earlier decision, and held that separate but equal was not a just law.

The *Brown v. Board of Education* decision was an extremely important turning point for blacks striving for the civil rights that were supposed to be guaranteed under the Bill of Rights. Indeed, by the time Al Sharpton found himself immersed in the civil rights movement in the 1960s, blacks had suffered through a long struggle to win the freedoms

The Supreme Court's decision in the case of Brown v. Board of Education of Topeka *in 1954 was a major first step in the fight for African-American civil rights. Thurgood Marshall (center) led a team of NAACP colleagues, including George E. C. Hayes (left) and James Nabrit (right), in the court victory.*

many Americans had long taken for granted.

As America moved into the 1950s, things began to change radically in the fight for African Americans. Civil rights groups that had called for racial equality for years now at least had the attention of the people. The most prominent of these groups, the National Association for the Advancement of Colored People, was pivotal in winning the *Brown v. Board of Education* case in 1954. Another civil rights group, the Congress of Racial Equality, founded in 1942, began a series of demonstrations and sit-ins during the 1950s, demanding that blacks be seated in white-only restaurants and similar places. Not all of CORE's work was limited to the South. CORE staged demonstrations against a whites-only swimming pool in Palisades, New Jersey, and whites-only restaurants in Baltimore, Maryland, and St. Louis, Missouri.

On December 1, 1955, a black seamstress named Rosa Parks stepped onto a crowded bus in Montgomery, Alabama. Parks was on her way home after a weary day at work. She found a seat on the bus, but a few minutes later a white man boarded the bus and demanded that she give up her seat for him—a common occurrence on Montgomery buses. The bus driver stopped the bus and summoned a police officer, who arrested Parks. She was soon bailed out of jail by a local leader of the NAACP.

Word of the arrest spread throughout the black community in Montgomery as well as elsewhere. Black leaders met at the Dexter Avenue Baptist Church in Montgomery and planned a boycott of the Montgomery bus system. No black would ride a bus in Montgomery until the city's bus company ensured that blacks would be just as entitled to seats as whites. The black leaders who met at Dexter Avenue Baptist that night also elected a minister to lead what would become known as the Montgomery Bus Boycott. That minister was the Reverend Dr. Martin Luther King Jr.

"My friends, we are here for serious business," King told black leaders gathered in the church that night. "We are here in a general sense because first and foremost, we are American citizens, and we are determined to acquire our citizenship to the fullness of its meaning. We are here because of our deep-seated belief that democracy transformed from thin paper to thick action is the greatest form of government on earth. But we are here in

One of the most pivotal events in the civil rights movement was the 1956 Montgomery bus boycott, initiated by Rosa Parks, who was arrested for refusing to give up her bus seat for white passengers. Here, Parks is fingerprinted by a deputy sheriff.

a specific sense because of the bus situation in Montgomery. We are here because we are determined to get the situation corrected."

Historians regard Rosa Park's arrest and the subsequent bus boycott as the beginning of the modern civil rights movement in America. It would also later serve as the model of protest for activists like Al Sharpton. During the boycott, Montgomery's 40,000 black citizens stayed off the city's buses for more than a year. They either walked to work, caught rides in car pools organized by black leaders, or received transportation from volunteers sympathetic to their plight.

The city wouldn't budge. As the months dragged on, the bus company remained segregated. Finally, though, the case was brought to the U.S. Supreme Court, which ordered the bus system in Montgomery desegregated. Blacks had stayed off the Montgomery buses for 382 days. The bus company in Montgomery lost hundreds of thousands of dollars.

"A miracle had taken place," King wrote after the boycott ended. "The once dormant and quiescent Negro community was now fully awake."

Blacks returned to the Montgomery buses on December 21, 1956. They now had the right to sit on a bus in a major American city. The Civil Rights Movement picked up a lot of steam, as less than 16 years later, Shirley Chisholm, a black congresswoman from New York City, would launch a candidacy for president.

Even before he finished high school, Al Sharpton had thrown himself fully into the Chisholm campaign. She campaigned hard in several Democratic primaries in the spring of 1972, but was never able to break through as one of the top-tier contenders for her party's nomination. Her share of the popular vote in the primaries never exceeded 7 percent. Still, she earned about 150

Longtime friend and mentor James Brown walks with Sharpton from a meeting at the White House in 1982.

delegates to the 1972 Democratic National Convention in Miami.

Sharpton returned to New York City, where he enrolled in Brooklyn College and majored in political science. Sharpton had his plate full with the National Youth Movement, and so left college early to devote more time to the organization. He also continued to socialize with prominent figures, and it was at that time that he became close with James Brown. Years before, when

Sharpton had lived in Queens, he had gotten to know the soul singer casually; they had lived in the same neighborhood. Brown was then a rising star on the music scene, years away from his status as a major recording artist known as the "Godfather of Soul."

In 1973, Sharpton went to a James Brown concert in Newark, New Jersey, and with the help of a friend was able to go backstage and meet Brown. During his visit, Sharpton told the singer about his efforts to organize the National Youth Movement. Brown pledged his support and promised to perform some benefit shows at the old Albee Theater in Brooklyn to raise money for the organization. Both shows sold out, which excited Brown. At the time, his career had slowed and he was having trouble filling seats. The night of the first National Youth Movement concert, James Brown and Al Sharpton became like father and son. Soon, the singer invited Sharpton to travel with him on tour as part of his staff, helping to promote his shows. They spent most of 1973 together.

Since Brown was 25 years his elder, Sharpton would always view his friend as a father: "He would talk to me the way a father talked to a son: 'Watch this on the road, don't deal with these kind of girls, dress like this, eat this.' I mean, literally like a father. And I guess because I never had that kind of relationship with anybody, he became the father I never had."

Indeed, for the rest of the 1970s, James Brown and Al Sharpton were inseparable, with Sharpton doing most of the organizational and promotional work for the Godfather of Soul. On July 4, 1974, Sharpton promoted a James Brown concert at Madison Square Garden in New York City that sold out to nearly 20,000 fans.

Meanwhile, Sharpton kept up his activities as head of the National Youth Movement. One early confrontation led to a Sharpton-led sit-in at the city's Department of Manpower to demand more summer jobs for African-American kids. Mayor Ed Koch refused to buckle under to the protest and instead called in the police to haul off the demonstrators. Now 19 years old and no longer a kid, Sharpton was taken into custody along with several other protesters. It was the first time Sharpton was arrested as the leader of a protest. It would be far from his last arrest.

Later that year, Brown was invited to perform in the Republic of the Congo in Africa at a concert staged shortly before the world heavyweight championship fight between Muhammad Ali and George Foreman. Back then, the country was known as Zaire. Sharpton went along, and during his trip to Zaire he met Don King, the colorful promoter of the fight later called the "Rumble in the Jungle."

King, who would become a close associate of Sharpton's, was one of the most flamboyant figures in American sports. King had come up the hard way—he had been a minor criminal in Cleveland, Ohio, who served a jail sentence for manslaughter. After his release from prison, King started promoting fights, and was the first black promoter to sign major boxing stars, most of whom were black. He is known for his wild hairdo—his hair seems to stand on end—his flashy jewelry, and his colorful talk. In the years to come, Don King and Al Sharpton would discover that their business and political interests often coincide.

Meanwhile, while on tour with James Brown, Sharpton met his future wife, Kathy Jordan, one of Brown's backup singers. He also started wearing his hair straight and combed in waves, just like James Brown styled his hair. Sharpton and Brown made a pact to always style their hair that way.

In 1981, Sharpton decided to leave Brown's side

so that he could devote all his energies to the National Youth Movement. He led protests against the city's Metropolitan Transit Authority, staging a sit-in on subway tracks to protest the racist hiring practices of the organization. He marched on City Hall to demand that a minority be named city schools chancellor—the highest position in the administration of the New York City schools. That protest was successful: it led to the hiring of Anthony Alvarado, a Latino.

While Al Sharpton was busy leading protesters on the streets of New York, young people everywhere were riveted by an incandescent black singer who had the whole country "moonwalking." His name was Michael Jackson, and his hit album "Thriller" had sold several million copies—a record that was surpassed only by The Eagles' *Greatest Hits (1971–1975)*.

In 1984 Jackson and his brothers—formerly the Jackson 5—were preparing for a 43-city concert series called the Victory Tour. Michael Jackson desperately wanted to include a black promoter on the tour—somebody who could arrange inner-city meetings between the Jacksons and their black fans. Michael was concerned that the tour would draw just white audiences, and that the Jacksons would appear to be turning their backs on their black fans. Don King, the tour producer, approached Sharpton and asked him to accompany the Jacksons across country. The Jacksons gave Sharpton a $500,000 budget and a four-person staff to arrange promotional visits by the Jacksons to black neighborhoods.

At each stop on the tour, Sharpton hired young black people to work at the concert sites. He gave out free tickets to black children and diffused tensions and boycotts when local black leaders complained that the tickets were too expensive for young black fans to afford.

For years promoter Don King has been an established figure in boxing and entertainment. In 1984, King asked Sharpton to help promote the Jackson brothers' national tour.

The Victory Tour was Sharpton's last experience in show business. But by no means would it be his last experience in front of the cameras. Just two years later, after another death arising out of racial hatred, Americans would be turning on their television sets to see Al Sharpton dominate the evening news programs for months.

4

HOWARD BEACH

❦

Sharpton takes his familiar position in front of a large group of demonstrators. Here, he leads a protest march in Howard Beach, Queens, over the murder of Michael Griffith in 1986.

$\mathbf{A}$FTER RETURNING FROM the Victory Tour, Sharpton threw himself back into activism, leading a National Youth Movement protest over the Bernhard Goetz case. A white subway rider, Goetz shot four black youths, claiming they had menaced him and that he feared for his life. Goetz received jail time for possession of the gun, but Sharpton and others believed he deserved a much heavier sentence. For months, the nation was divided on the issue of Bernhard Goetz and whether he was right to use deadly force.

Meanwhile, Sharpton organized a "War on Crack," vowing to drive out the drug dealers who sold the cheap cocaine derivative that was destroying so many young lives. Volunteers from the National Youth Movement went from neighborhood to neighborhood, painting the doors of so-called "crack houses" red. He also organized a fund-raising dinner for Daytop Village, a New York anti-drug program.

On December 20, 1986, Sharpton received a call from one of his volunteer crack house door painters named Derrick Jeter, who told Sharpton that his friend, Michael Griffith, 23, had been killed that night on a deserted stretch of the Belt Parkway in Howard Beach, Queens. During the incident that led to his death, Griffith was accompanied by his cousin,

Curtis Sylvester; his soon-to-be-stepfather, Cedric Sandiford; and a friend, Timmy Grimes. The four men had been searching for the home of Michael's employer to pick up his wages.

They had gotten lost and stopped at the New Park Pizza restaurant to use the phone. Within minutes, a white mob emerged from the pizza shop and confronted the black men. The mob chased Michael Griffith and the others for three blocks. As the young man fled in terror, he was struck by a car in the darkness of the Belt Parkway.

"It was like a thud, a thump—I could hear it from the end of the block," said Robert Riley, who would eventually testify against the assailants. "I saw his body go up a couple of feet in the air, above the car."

Sharpton recalled the phone call he received from Jeter. "He kept saying, 'They killed my friend out in Queens,' and then he asked me to call his friend's mother and go out and see her in Queens. . . . I decided to take the number and the address, and I told him that I'd go over in the morning and find out what had happened."

When Sharpton arrived the next day at the Griffith's, Cedric Sandiford, who had also been beaten by the mob, was there. His face still swollen from the punches he took, Sandiford told Sharpton the complete story. "He just sat there, bleeding from cuts and bruises with his clothes dirtied and torn," said Sharpton. "I became furious as I sat there listening to Cedric. And beyond anger I felt humiliation. . . . I was enraged. I told Mrs. Griffith and Cedric Sandiford that whatever we could do, they could count on us doing it. I had no idea what was possible, and I didn't know what, exactly, to do at that moment, but I knew we were going to do something."

Mayor Koch condemned the attack, announcing that the city would post a $10,000 reward for information leading to the arrest of the killers.

Sharpton didn't think that the reward was enough. He announced that the National Youth Movement would match what he regarded as the city's paltry reward.

Meanwhile, Michael Griffith's mother retained civil rights attorney Alton Maddox Jr. to represent her family. Together, Sharpton and Maddox would wage a stinging war of words against the city administration and law enforcement agencies until the assailants were brought to trial.

Sharpton made plans to lead a protest through Howard Beach. The protest took the form of a slow-moving motorcade that inched its way down the Belt Parkway. All along the route, angry people shouted taunts at Sharpton and the other protesters, demanding that they leave Howard Beach. The motorcade stopped in front of New Park Pizza. Sharpton got out of his car and stood in front of the pizza shop with other black activists, showing they had the right to walk into the neighborhood, and any neighborhood in the United States.

Sharpton stands with fellow protesters in front of New Park Pizza, where two months earlier Michael Griffith and three others were attacked by an angry white mob. The demonstrators hoped their protest would assure a just trial and help prevent similar attacks in the future.

"The taunts and insults from the crowd angered rather than frightened me," Sharpton said. "I looked at those enraged, contorted faces and I never thought about the danger."

Sharpton quickly made plans for a second Howard Beach protest—this time, it would take the form of a march through the all-white neighborhood scheduled for Saturday, December 27.

Thousands of people took part in the march. They trudged along two miles of the icy, windswept Cross Bay Boulevard in Queens. Marching at the head of the demonstration was Sharpton and Benjamin Hooks, executive director of the NAACP.

Meanwhile, Alton Maddox devised a legal strategy that would be repeated many times by black activists in years to come. Representing Cedric Sandiford—the main witness—Maddox advised his client not to cooperate with Queens authorities. Instead, Maddox demanded a special prosecutor appointed by the governor. Maddox believed that the prosecutors appointed by the Queens court would be too passive, and that fearing a political backlash from their white constituents, they would hesitate to press homicide charges against the assailants.

On December 27—the same day as the march through Howard Beach—Queens Supreme Court Judge Ernest Bianchi threw out murder, manslaughter, and assault charges against three Howard Beach men arrested in the case: Jon Lester, Scott Kern, and Jason Ladone. Without the testimony of Sandiford, the judge said, the prosecution could not possibly prove the charges. The judge recommended, though, that the three men be charged with a much less serious offense: reckless endangerment. Maddox renewed his call for a special prosecutor, and he promised that would be the only way authorities could expect Sandiford's cooperation.

For his part, Sharpton kept up the pressure, particularly on Mayor Koch. Whenever the mayor appeared in public, Sharpton made sure that the city leader was met by angry black protesters shouting, "No justice, no peace!"

Finally, on January 13, 1987, New York governor Mario Cuomo appointed Charles Hynes the special prosecutor in the Griffith case. Hynes was a former chief of the district attorney's rackets bureau in Brooklyn, and later District Attorney of Brooklyn.

Former New York mayor Ed Koch speaks at a press conference while Sharpton looks on. As mayor during the Howard Beach tragedy, Koch had condemned the attack, but Sharpton believed he had not been aggressive enough. In the months preceding the Howard Beach trial, Sharpton arrived with protesters wherever Koch made a public appearance.

Hynes didn't meet Mason's and Maddox's requirements, and so the protests didn't stop. On January 21, Sharpton led the "Day of Outrage," a demonstration involving 10,000 young black people on Fifth Avenue in Manhattan. The march ended in a rally in front of Mayor Koch's Greenwich Village apartment.

"So we marched and marched and marched, keeping the issues out there, deliberately provoking conflict and attention," Sharpton said.

Hynes announced the indictments on February 9. A dozen of the assailants faced charges. Hynes indicted four men on the most serious charges of manslaughter and murder. They were Lester, Kern, Ladone, and a fourth man, Michael Pirone.

The four men went on trial on September 8. Sharpton attended every session of the court proceedings. The prosecution took some seven weeks to present its case, calling 61 witnesses. The defense case was simple: the black men—not the whites—had begun the altercation by flashing knives, and the white group's retaliation had ended by the time Griffith was struck by the car.

The jury got the case on December 10, nearly a year after the incident. Every night of deliberations, Sharpton spoke at a candlelight vigil in front of the courthouse in Queens. On December 20, the anniversary of Griffith's death, Sharpton led a memorial service at Our Lady of Charity Church in Queens.

"Every child in these United States will be told a story, as Michael's mother was told, about 'bringing me your huddled masses yearning to be free,'" Sharpton told the people gathered in the church, referring to the message inscribed at the base of the Statue of Liberty. "And when she came, and when her son came down to get a paycheck, the Statue of Liberty wasn't holding no light for Michael.

"But we're gonna raise that light up if it takes

all the strength in our arms; we're gonna make justice reign even if it costs us our very life. We will not let you down Michael, because some of us would rather die on our feet than keep standing on our knees."

For weeks, Sharpton had been planning a second Day of Outrage, but city officials feared the event would lead to racial violence, so they won a court order barring the protest. Sharpton decided to defy the court order and carry out the demonstration. He planned to lead a blockade of the bridges leading into Manhattan the next day, December 21. Sharpton called a press conference and, looking into the TV cameras, defiantly tore up the court order.

Things started happening very quickly. On December 21, as Sharpton and the protesters were planning the Day of Outrage, the jury suddenly returned a verdict. The jury elected not to convict on murder charges, but Lester, Kern, and Ladone were found guilty of manslaughter in the second degree—a lesser charge that is not subject to the death penalty or life imprisonment. Pirone was found not guilty on all charges.

"Murderers!" shouted protesters in the courtroom, who were quickly dragged away by court officers.

Black protesters poured into the streets; hundreds made their way into the subway stations. One station hit hard by the protesters was the subway stop below Brooklyn Borough Hall—hundreds jammed onto the railway platform. Some of the young demonstrators forced their way into trains and disabled the vehicles by pulling the emergency brake cords. That day, a significant portion of New York City's mass transit system ground to a halt.

Sharpton and other black leaders joined in the protest, stepping onto subway tracks and forcing trains to come to a standstill. That scene was repeated at other stations. "No justice, no peace!" shouted

On December 21, 1987, a jury returned a verdict that found the three defendants in the Howard Beach case guilty of manslaughter. Angry that the verdicts were not stronger, Sharpton and dozens of others spilled onto the tracks of a New York subway station in protest, shutting down four major subway lines for several hours.

the protesters. At one subway station, 100 black youths linked arms and refused to move, even when confronted by helmeted riot police.

"This is a monumental occasion," said Alton Maddox. "This is a beginning of a civil rights movement in the city of New York. We're sick and tired of the law being used against us."

Seventy-three protesters were arrested, including Sharpton. "This is just the beginning," said the Reverend Benjamin Chavis Jr., a minister who was also among the protest leaders arrested. "This city will never be the same after this day. We serve notice on all those in power that your days are numbered."

Despite the outrage exhibited by many black leaders, Sharpton was not entirely displeased with the verdicts. He expressed his satisfaction that Lester, Kern, and Ladone would receive significant jail terms.

"For the first time, whites were going to do serious time for assaulting a black in a bias case in New York City," Sharpton said. "Black lives were worth something in the eyes of the law."

5

WAPPINGERS FALLS

❧

THE HOWARD BEACH case proved to be a watershed event in the life of the Reverend Al Sharpton: he was no longer considered just a young upstart; Sharpton was now a player and political force in the events of the nation's largest city. Indeed, Sharpton had proved he could mobilize thousands of citizens and direct their energies toward addressing the social injustice he believed was still very much a part of the fabric of American society.

But in 1987 the Tawana Brawley case would demonstrate that public figures with Sharpton's degree of notoriety must act prudently if they wish to maintain their reputations. The story begins in Wappingers Falls, a small town on the Hudson River, some 65 miles north of New York City. The village gets its name from the scenic waterfalls that carry Wappingers Creek on its way to the Hudson. The town was built around some old mills that operated for decades, powered by the rushing waters of Wappingers Creek, but are now out of commission. Today, all that is left of those old mills is some stone and brick remnants.

But life goes on in Wappingers Falls. Located in Dutchess County, the town of just 5,000 people hosts the Great Hudson Valley Balloon Race and Air Show. There are two fire stations in Wappingers Falls—the oldest was founded in 1869.

Tawana Brawley speaks at a press conference, flanked by her attorney, Alton Maddox Jr. (left), and Sharpton. While the court and much of the public would remain skeptical about her alleged kidnapping and rape, Sharpton continued to staunchly defend her.

Wappingers Falls hardly sounds like the type of place where one would encounter racial violence. But after what occurred on the night of November 24, 1987, the people of Wappingers Falls would learn a lot about the issues that can fuel the hatred between the races.

That night a black teenager named Tawana Brawley was found naked and wrapped in a plastic trash bag behind a Wappingers Falls apartment complex. She claimed to have been beaten and raped; what's more, dog feces was smeared on her body and the letters "KKK"—the initials for the racist organization the Ku Klux Klan—scrawled on her skin.

The 15-year-old told police she had been returning home by bus after visiting a former boyfriend in the Orange County jail. She got off the bus a mile from her home at about 8:30 P.M. on November 24. As she walked down the road, a sedan pulled up and a sandy-haired white man with a mustache showed her a badge and gun and told her to get into the car. Tawana later reported that there was one more man in the car. She screamed for police, but was told by the man, "Shut up, stupid, I am a police officer."

Tawana said she was then struck on the head with the gun and knocked unconscious. Later, she awoke in the woods, surrounded by six white men. She thought she had been drugged, and lapsed in and out of consciousness for the next four days.

"I cannot describe the horror I felt upon hearing the full details of this story," said Sharpton. "No black person is without historical memory of the outrages visited upon black women throughout slavery and into the 20th Century. I was interested in this case because I thought someone had to stand up and defend this young girl; I felt like I was defending my mother, my wife, my daughters, my sisters, all the black women I know and love."

The story had come to Sharpton's attention

through Lillian Howard, an NAACP leader in Newburgh, New York, which is close to Wappingers Falls. Sharpton flew into action in his typical style: he decided to stage a rally on December 12, 1987, at a church in Newburgh.

"We're in a state of emergency in the state of New York," Sharpton told more than 1,000 people who jammed into the Newburgh Baptist Temple that night. Later, Sharpton led a march through the streets of Newburgh. One of the black leaders who marched alongside Sharpton was Louis Farrakhan, head of the black religious organization known as the Nation of Islam.

Sharpton was also joined at the rally by Alton Maddox, who had been Cedric Sandiford's lawyer in the Howard Beach case. Sharpton and Maddox met with Tawana's mother, Glenda Brawley, and the girl's stepfather, Ralph King. The family quickly agreed to

Attorneys C. Vernon Mason (second from left) and Alton Maddox Jr. (far right) join Sharpton in leading a protest through a New York City street. Sharpton was arrested later that day, and at the end of 1988 would face further legal disputes when he was indicted with fraud, larceny, and tax evasion.

be represented by Maddox and another attorney from the Howard Beach case, C. Vernon Mason.

There were now three black leaders standing out front of the Brawley family in every turn of the case: Maddox and Mason would handle the legal strategies and Sharpton would serve as family spokesman, chief rabble-rouser, and self-appointed lightning rod for the criticism he knew would be aimed at the Brawleys.

Police began by combing through the few clues available to them. Their suspicions fell first on Ralph King, who was on parole after serving 11 years in prison for the fatal shooting of his wife.

But then Timothy Losee, a letter carrier, reported that he saw a police cruiser carrying four white men driving through the Brawleys' apartment complex on November 28, the day Tawana was found. Next, on December 1, a part-time police officer named Harry Crist committed suicide, shortly after he told investigators he had been riding around with New York State Trooper Scott Patterson on the night of the abduction. Crist's car was a decommissioned police cruiser, and it fit the description given to investigators by the letter carrier. Patterson and a Dutchess County assistant district attorney named Steven Pagones became the chief suspects in the case. Pagones and Crist had been good friends.

When Pagones' name surfaced as a suspect, Dutchess County district attorney William Grady announced he would withdraw from the case, citing a conflict of interest. That gave Maddox, Mason, and Sharpton cause to demand a special prosecutor, just as they had demanded in the Howard Beach case. And they insisted that Tawana would refuse to cooperate until Governor Mario Cuomo met their demands.

Cuomo soon found himself under more pressure to appoint a special prosecutor. TV star Bill Cosby stepped forward and posted a $25,000 reward for information leading to the arrest of the

suspects. Mike Tyson, the heavyweight boxer, gave Tawana a watch valued at $30,000. Boxing promoter Don King pledged $100,000 to set up a fund for Tawana's education.

On January 26, 1988, Cuomo stepped forward, appointing New York attorney general Robert Abrams special prosecutor in the case. "As far as I am concerned, Tawana Brawley is my daughter—she is everybody's daughter," Cuomo said. "We will do everything we can to get at the truth."

Abrams was a much-respected lawyer and a noted civil libertarian—he had a reputation for fighting for the rights of the individual. But Sharpton did not believe that the white lawyer could commit fully to the case, and Sharpton and the others complained bitterly. Sharpton also charged that Abrams would use the Brawley case to advance his own political agenda.

Steven Pagones, an assistant district attorney, was accused of abducting and raping Tawana Brawley in 1987. Pagones was later cleared of all charges when a grand jury declared Brawley's story a hoax. He retaliated by filing a $150 million civil suit against Mason, Maddox, and Sharpton.

"I was worried that the attorney general's office would try to score points with the public to build Abrams' political profile," Sharpton said. "That was very disturbing, given that this was the most sensitive bias case in New York State history. I think there became times the authorities were as interested in nailing Sharpton, Maddox and Mason as they were in finding out what happened to that girl those four days."

If Abrams' target was really Al Sharpton, he wasn't the only one hunting for Sharpton's scalp. On January 20, 1988, the New York newspaper *Newsday* started publishing a series of articles naming Sharpton as a secret informant for the Federal Bureau of Investigation. Throughout its history, the FBI has often approached private citizens who may have valuable information of criminal activities. Sometimes, the FBI has gone beyond its crime fighting duties to keep a close eye on civil rights leaders and other activists who challenge the status quo. In Sharpton's case, according to the newspaper, he had been "secretly supplying law enforcement agencies with information on boxing promoter Don King, reputed organized crime figures and black elected officials."

Sharpton admitted giving some information to the FBI, but contended that his assistance to the agency was minimal. "Under normal circumstances, if someone works with the government, provides information useful to the apprehension of criminals, he's a hero," said Sharpton. "It remains extremely suspicious to me that I was suddenly set up as an informer—not only on drug dealers, which I've freely admitted, but on black activists and politicians."

Sharpton insisted that his political enemies had leaked the story to *Newsday* in an attempt to discredit him during the Brawley investigation. Sharpton, Maddox, and Mason shot back, turning up the heat on Abrams with fiery rhetoric of their own.

"The authorities haven't focused on this case as a rape-kidnap because it involves a black woman," said Mason. "There is no equal protection under the law when it comes to us. . . .We had death after death after death and never a conviction."

In February, Abrams took the Brawley case before a grand jury. Prosecutors often use grand juries to help them investigate crimes. The panels are composed of ordinary citizens who meet in secret, hearing testimony from witnesses who may be reluctant to step forward to tell what they know. By meeting in secret, the witnesses usually feel freer to discuss the case, knowing their identities will be protected. But grand juries can go further to investigate a case—they have subpoena power, which means they can force reluctant witnesses to appear before them and tell what they know. A subpoena is a court order that compels a reluctant witness to

New York attorney general Robert Abrams (center) was assigned as special prosecutor to the Brawley case, but Sharpton, Maddox, and Mason didn't trust him. Abrams, who suffered much public criticism from Sharpton and others during the 1988 trial, later fought back by organizing a grand jury investigation of Sharpton, and by legally pursuing Maddox and Mason.

(From left) Mason, Sharpton, and Maddox speak to reporters in front of the Ebenezer Baptist Church in Queens, where they hid Glenda Brawley, mother of Tawana Brawley, from authorities. As in the Howard Beach case a year earlier, Maddox and his witnesses refused to heed the court subpoenas until a special prosecutor could be agreed upon.

testify before a grand jury or, if necessary, in open court. Abrams aimed to use the powers of the grand jury to get to the bottom of the Brawley case.

One of the witnesses he asked to appear before the grand jury was Tawana's mother, Glenda. Maddox and Mason, still pursuing their strategy of keeping witnesses from cooperating with investigators, advised Glenda Brawley not to testify. Abrams issued a subpoena for Glenda Brawley; Mason and Maddox responded by hiding Glenda in the Ebenezer Baptist Church in Brooklyn. Mason, Maddox, and Sharpton insisted that Abrams had no intention of presenting fair and truthful evidence before the grand jury; they demanded that a new special prosecutor be appointed, or that federal authorities take over the case and impanel their own grand jury. Sharpton even ripped up Glenda's subpoena in front of TV cameras.

When Judge Angelo Ingrassia insisted that Glenda testify or serve 30 days in jail on a contempt charge, Sharpton and the others moved her to another church.

"My lawyers did explain that this is for all black people," Glenda told reporters.

Next, Perry McKinnon entered the fray. McKinnon had been Sharpton's assistant, but quit because he started to doubt Tawana's story. Indeed, McKinnon told reporters that the charges leveled by Sharpton, Maddox, and Mason at Abrams and the other authorities were little more than a "pack of lies." He even said to one TV reporter: "I'm not going with a fraud."

Sharpton, Maddox, and Mason had told reporters they had proof white law enforcement officers raped Tawana, but McKinnon said no such evidence existed. According to McKinnon, Maddox had once disclosed, "I don't care about no facts. I'm not going to pursue it legally; I'm going to pursue it politically."

Said McKinnon: "This case is not about Tawana, it's about Mason, Maddox and Sharpton taking over the town, so to speak." He called the three Brawley family advisers "hustlers and crooks."

Sharpton countered that McKinnon had just briefly worked for him, and that his real goal was to become a private security consultant with big-time clients, and that he had begged Sharpton to introduce him to such wealthy people as Don King and tycoon Donald Trump.

"This was his attempt to get attention, and probably get even, in his mind, with me," said Sharpton.

The year dragged on. Sharpton found himself confronted with other dilemmas. He faced charges stemming from the resistance he helped stir up to protest the Howard Beach verdicts. In 1993, after exhausting his appeals, Sharpton was finally sentenced to 25 days in New York's tough Rikers Island Prison.

In October 1988, Robert Abrams released the report of the grand jury. The investigation concluded that Tawana Brawley had not been abducted and raped; Steven Pagones and Scott Patterson were cleared of all suspicion. Investigators concluded that Tawana had stayed out all night and, fearing trouble from her parents, made up a story and hoped that the charge of racism would protect her. The grand jury concluded that Tawana and her three advisers had perpetrated a hoax.

Although the grand jury had issued its report, the case was far from over. Abrams filed a complaint in court against Maddox, whose license to practice law was eventually suspended. Mason was charged with obstructing the investigation and making false statements about the case, and he lost his license to practice law as well. And the attorney general impaneled a new grand jury—this time to investigate Sharpton; soon, the reverend found himself charged with 67 counts of fraud and larceny and additional charges for tax evasion. In the first case, Sharpton was cleared of all 67 charges. A circuit court judge ordered the tax evasion charges dropped because of double jeopardy. In other words, the court could not pursue the matter since Sharpton had been cleared of the previous charges. Eventually, the court issued Sharpton a small fine for failing to file a New York State personal income tax return for 1986.

The legal entanglements continued. Pagones filed a $150 million lawsuit against Sharpton, Maddox, and Mason, charging that they intentionally lied when they accused him of participating in the rape of Tawana Brawley. The case went to trial in 1997, and resulted in verdicts against the three Brawley family advisers. The lawsuit resulted in monetary damages assessed against Sharpton, Maddox, and Mason.

Pagones won far less than the $150 million he had sought; still, Sharpton found himself responsible for paying $66,000 to the former Dutchess County assistant district attorney.

For Al Sharpton, the Brawley case led to an investigation into his finances by the New York attorney general in addition to a court award in the Pagones lawsuit. But his fierce defense of Tawana Brawley cost him much more than just money: he emerged from the Tawana Brawley case with a somewhat tarnished reputation.

Sharpton continues to stand by Tawana Brawley, as well as his own involvement in the case. "I think if I had to do it again I'd do it the same way," Sharpton said. "I probably wouldn't have gotten into such a personal contest with Robert Abrams, but I would do the whole thing again."

He also believed that many people misunderstood the court's decision: "I think people might like to explain my ferocious involvement as overemotional zeal, but the fact is, Tawana was never disproved. Can I say that I know beyond a shadow of a doubt what happened? No. Neither can my critics. We haven't proved anything definitively, but it hasn't been dismissed. Who has conclusively proven her to be false? Not Abrams, not the FBI, not Dutchess County."

6

"CLOUDS OF VIOLENCE"

❦

ANYBODY WHO READ author Tom Wolfe's book *Bonfire of the Vanities*, published in 1987, or saw the movie version starring Tom Hanks and Bruce Willis, couldn't help but notice the character of Reverend Bacon: a portly, loud-mouthed street preacher who delightfully stirs up trouble in a racially-charged hit-and-run incident in New York City.

There was no question that Wolfe based the boisterous Reverend Bacon on Reverend Sharpton. In the aftermath of the Brawley case, Sharpton's controversial reputation plunged, especially with the media. Among critical reporters, he earned a nickname: Reverend Soundbite. A soundbite is a term TV reporters use for the few seconds of videotape filmed at a news event that can be edited into the nightly newscast. Reporters knew that Sharpton could always be counted on to provide a juicy quote—a soundbite—they could use on the evening news.

Nevertheless, Sharpton was little troubled by his less than sparkling portrayal in books, movies, and the press. Indeed, in late 1989, less than a year after the Brawley verdict, Sharpton once again found himself defending the rights of African-American victims of racial violence.

The Bensonhurst case was certainly a legitimate

Sharpton poses with 60 Minutes correspondent Mike Wallace. Sharpton, nicknamed "Reverend Soundbite," has through the years drawn a great deal of controversy for using the media to expose important issues.

71

case. On August 23, 1989, Yusuf Hawkins was fatally shot in the Brooklyn neighborhood; the 16-year-old high school student and two friends had been attacked by a white mob.

Sharpton would again throw himself into a racially-charged incident; only this time, he would pay with more than just his pocketbook or reputation. This time, he would put his life on the line.

■   ■   ■

It had all been a misunderstanding, police later learned. Some local toughs had confronted a white girl and her black boyfriend. They told her to find another boyfriend. To get them to back off, she threatened that her boyfriend and others would deal with them. The day was muggy, temperatures were high and so were emotions. Angry words were exchanged. Moments later, Yusuf and his friends had the misfortune to wander into the scene. The mob, worked into a frenzy of racial hatred, took them for the boyfriend and his crew and surrounded them. A gun went off. Yusuf was killed, dead of a gunshot wound to his heart.

Yusuf's family was devastated and wanted to take some kind of action in response to the senseless killing. "The day after the shooting took place in Bensonhurst, we were in front of my home at 485 Hegemann Avenue, and there was a gob of reporters outside the house," said Moses Stewart, Yusuf's father. "Someone out of the crowd yelled, 'If there was someone that you could call to help you in your plight, you and your family, who would you call?'

"So I told them that if there was anyone that I would call, it would be the likes of the Rev. Al Sharpton or Minister Louis Farrakhan. That's how it got out, and then one of the reporters handed me Sharpton's phone number. And I ended up calling him—the same day, as a matter of fact."

Sharpton arrived at Yusuf Hawkins's home to find it surrounded by TV trucks. He waded through the crowd of reporters, pushing his way past microphones and tape recorders thrust in his face. From the mouths of Yusuf's parents, Moses Stewart and Diane Hawkins, Sharpton heard the story of how their son had lost his life.

During his meeting with the boy's parents, the family received an unexpected visit from David Dinkins—Sharpton's old ally from the National Youth Movement. Following their work together in the organization, Sharpton and Dinkins had gone their separate ways: Sharpton into activism, Dinkins into politics. After serving as attorney for the National Youth Movement, Dinkins won elective office as Manhattan Borough president. He was now a candidate for mayor of New York City.

Sharpton believed Dinkins had pushed his way into the Stewart-Hawkins home to draw the spotlight away from the grieving family, and onto his own candidacy for mayor. But Sharpton kept his cool, and let Dinkins bask in the press attention.

"He went outside and made his statement and left, and I think we helped him there, because if a black family that had suffered such a devastating tragedy at the hands of whites had come out and publicly denounced Dinkins and accused him of betraying them, he would have lost the black community and the election," Sharpton said.

In fact, that November Dinkins went on to win the mayor's race, becoming the first African American to head the government of the nation's largest city.

Inside the house, the phone never seemed to stop ringing. Governor Mario Cuomo and Jesse Jackson both called, pledging to help raise money for the funeral expenses. New York Mayor Ed Koch also pledged to find money to help the family. But

Sharpton wanted to make sure Cuomo and Koch paid attention to the Bensonhurst case long after Yusuf was buried. "We had to assert the right of blacks to be anywhere in the city, to come and go as they pleased as law-abiding taxpayers without fear or apprehension," Sharpton said. "It had gone on too long in New York City that blacks were limited in their travel, and worst of all, it was as if nothing had been learned from Howard Beach.

"As long as I can remember, that had been how it was in Bensonhurst, that any black person who went there was taking his or her life in his or her own hands, even in daylight. Someone would stumble in there by accident, get lost or something, then get beat up, hurt, and no one, not the mayor, not the police, not mainstream black leaders, ever said anything." Meanwhile, police looked into the case and eventually charged eight people with participating in the attack. As the defendants approached trial Sharpton spoke out publicly, calling for murder convictions. To keep the heat on the authorities, Sharpton orchestrated 29 marches and protest rallies in Bensonhurst from August 1989 until January 1991.

By early 1990, Sharpton predicted wide-scale violence in New York City unless the killers of Yusuf Hawkins were convicted and sentenced to the maximum penalties under law.

"Don't blame me," Sharpton warned a reporter. "As a social weatherman, I'm telling you that the clouds of violence are over New York City."

On January 12, 1991, the Bensonhurst case would erupt in violence—but it would occur much closer to Sharpton than he anticipated. That was the day Michael Riccardi made his way through the crowd in the playground at Public School 205 and thrust a knife into Sharpton's chest.

Of the eight people tried in the attack on Yusuf Hawkins, three went to prison, two were convicted

Like Sharpton, former New York City mayor David Dinkins was a member of the National Youth Movement. At the time of the Bensonhurst attack, Dinkins was running for mayor and publicly pledged his support to Yusuf Hawkins' family.

of minor offenses and given probation, and three were found not guilty.

One of the men convicted in the case, Keith Mondello, was released from prison in May 1998. Mondello admitted being a ringleader of the mob that had surrounded Yusuf. He was acquitted of a murder charge, but found guilty of rioting, unlawful imprisonment, and possession of a weapon.

Mondello was released on parole after serving eight years of a 12-year sentence. Shortly after he

Ten years after the death of his son Yusuf Hawkins, Moses Stewart returned with Sharpton to the site of the murder. Here, Stewart prays with the minister after putting down a memorial wreath of flowers.

walked out of jail, Sharpton organized a rally in Bensonhurst to protest Mondello's parole. About 150 people marched through the Brooklyn neighborhood on June 6, 1998. Moses Stewart led the march as protesters repeated the now-familiar chant of "No justice, no peace!"

Later, Stewart told a reporter that he believes the threat of racial violence remains a part of life in America.

"Can I sleep at night a little better?" Stewart said on the 10th anniversary of his son's death. "Yes. Has some of the rage in me calmed? Yes. As far as me being peaceful about the racial overtones— no. I am still just as up in arms as the day after my son died."

7

CROWN HEIGHTS

❦

THROUGHOUT AMERICAN HISTORY, Jews had often found themselves the victims of the same type of ethnic prejudice and stereotyping that afflicted blacks. For Jews, though, the prejudice was often more subtle. While blacks often found "Whites Only" signs on the entrances to restaurants and railroad stations, Jews were often turned down for admittance to colleges, country clubs, and fraternal organizations with no explanations. Of course, the meaning had been made clear: they weren't allowed to join because they were Jews.

And so, over the years blacks and Jews have found themselves with common goals: the quest for social justice, the elimination of bigotry, and the adoption of laws prohibiting segregation.

Certainly, there were times when their paths crossed and they united to achieve these goals. In the 1700s and 1800s, African slaves read the Old Testament of the Bible—a sacred text of Judaism—and found comfort in the story of Moses, who led the Jewish people out of slavery in Egypt to establish a homeland in Israel.

In 1909, Jewish Americans helped blacks organize the NAACP. Jewish philanthropists sent money to the South to help educate thousands of illiterate black children. In the 1930s, Jews and blacks flocked to join the Democratic Party, drawn by the strong message of inclusion offered by President Franklin D. Roosevelt. In

1947, black American diplomat Ralph Bunche, who had helped write the charter for the United Nations, negotiated the peace that ended the Arab-Israeli war and helped establish the modern nation of Israel. Bunche would later be awarded the Nobel Peace Prize for his efforts. And in the 1960s, many young Jewish students worked as "freedom riders," traveling throughout the South to help register blacks to vote. One of those freedom riders was U.S. senator Joseph Lieberman of Connecticut, who in 2000 would become the first Jew to win a place on a national presidential ticket when he ran for vice president.

But although there have been examples of how blacks and Jews have worked together over the years to fight prejudice, there have been many times when relations between the two ethnic groups have been strained. Poor blacks in the cities often found themselves at the mercy of Jewish shopkeepers and landlords, who decided when and when not to advance credit to their customers. Blacks would bristle when they heard the word "shvartzer"—a Yiddish term of ridicule aimed at black people.

In 1979, black civil rights activist Andrew Young resigned as the United States representative to the United Nations when it was revealed he held secret negotiations with leaders of the Palestine Liberation Organization; at the time the group was composed of terrorists who had sworn to eliminate the State of Israel. Although the PLO eventually became less ruthless and its leaders helped negotiate a framework for a separate Palestinian state in the Middle East, at the time the United States had no diplomatic relations with the PLO. American Jews were angered at Young's willingness to meet with people regarded then as the sworn enemies of Israel.

At one time, the Reverend Jesse Jackson helped fan the flames as well. During a visit to the Middle East Jackson met with and embraced PLO leader Yasir Arafat. In his campaign for the presidency in 1984,

President Truman presents African-American diplomat Dr. Ralph Bunche (right) with an Outstanding Citizenship Award in 1949. Bunche's work in helping establish the modern nation of Israel exemplifies the bond between Jewish Americans and African Americans who have recognized their common hardships as victims of discrimination.

Jackson courted votes from Arab Americans, spoke out against "Jewish slumlords" in New York and, in a fit of anger, used the derogatory term "Hymies" for Jews and referred to New York as "Hymietown."

However, Jackson later admitted that he regretted having made the racial epithets. He resolved to become more tolerant of all races and also issued a formal apology:

"If in my low moments, in word, deed, or attitude, through some error of temper, taste, or tone, I have caused any discomfort, created pain, or revived someone's fears, that was not my truest self. As I develop and serve, be patient. God is not finished with me yet." Jackson's words served as evidence that between Jews and African Americans, there was some hope. And then came Crown Heights.

■   ■   ■

One of Judaism's most orthodox and devout sects is the Hasidim—a group of Jews known for their

Reverend Jesse Jackson embraces Yasir Arafat, leader of the Palestinian Liberation Organization, at a 1979 meeting in Beirut. Jackson's friendly relations with the Arab leader angered many Jewish-Americans. Things would get even worse in 1984 when Jackson used racial epithets in speaking out against Jewish slumlords, a blunder for which he later made a public apology.

conservative clothes, long beards, old-country ways and strict devotion to prayer. They also closely observe religious customs of the Sabbath, the period from sundown Friday to sundown Saturday that Jews regard as the holiest time of the week. During the early part of the 20th Century, the center for Hasidim was Eastern Europe and Russia, but thousands of Hasidic Jews were killed in the Holocaust during World War II. Many Hasidim escaped, and made their way to America; a number of those immigrants settled in the Brooklyn neighborhood of Crown Heights. For years, their spiritual leader was Rabbi Menachem Mendel Schneerson.

Starting in the 1960s, the Hasidim found themselves sharing Crown Heights with black neighbors; indeed, Al Sharpton had spent part of his childhood living in Crown Heights. Over the years, more and more blacks from the West Indies nations emigrated to the United States and made their homes in Crown

Heights. By the early 1990s, Crown Heights was home to a considerable population of blacks from Haiti, the Dominican Republic, Jamaica, and Guyana.

The West Indies blacks and Hasidic Jews were uneasy neighbors. "Crown Heights has always been a strange piece of the fabric of New York, populated as it is by a mixture of American and West Indian blacks and a significant concentration of Hasidic Jews," Sharpton said. "The blacks have long accused the Hasidim of receiving special treatment from the police, of cutting special property deals with the city—the city favoring the Hasidim for the purchase of lots and empty buildings—to increase their numbers, of blocking streets on the Sabbath, including the streets that house non-Hasidim, and of harassing blacks into giving up property that fits into Hasidic designs."

Sharpton described the Hasidic community as a "Fort Apache" within Crown Heights, an outpost protecting its inhabitants from a restless and hostile enemy. The community's situation is "always tense," he noted, but it is "usually quiet."

■   ■   ■

On the night of August 19, 1991, a seven-year-old Guyanese boy named Gavin Cato and his cousin Angela were playing in a Crown Heights street when the police-escorted motorcade of Rebbe Schneerson approached the intersection. What happened next was over in a few seconds. A vehicle approached from another direction; a car in the motorcade driven by Schneerson's assistant, Yosef Lifsh, swerved to avoid the collision, striking Gavin and his sister. Angela was severely injured; Gavin was killed. Gavin's father, Carmel Cato, arrived on the scene to find his son dead. A group of angry blacks who saw the accident pulled Lifsh out of his car and pounced on him. Police soon arrived to save Lifsh from the mob, but tempers remained high.

New York Post reporter Larry Celona wrote of accompanying police to the accident scene: "The swelling mob was yelling and screaming, and lines of riot-clad cops were trying to push them back from the corner of that tragic accident involving little Gavin Cato. The words of the mob were incomprehensible. The feeling was unmistakable: anger, frustration, hate. The next hours are a blur, with the events happening in quick and sickening waves. . . . The Crown Heights riot was the closest I'll ever come to being on the front line of a war."

Soon, the news of Gavin's death spread throughout Crown Heights, and riots broke out. When a young rabbinical student named Yankel Rosenbaum found himself cornered by a mob, he was attacked. As blacks shouted "Get the Jew!" a hand wielding a knife stabbed Rosenbaum, and he died as well.

Sharpton later wrote in his autobiography: "I will always be deeply sorry for what happened to Yankel Rosenbaum; it was the unfair and unfortunate murder of an innocent young man. And it was, for the black community, at best counterproductive, an unleashing of emotion that reduced that mob to the level of the killers in Howard Beach and Bensonhurst. We will not achieve justice behaving in the same exact ways as those we oppose."

The deaths of Gavin Cato and Yankel Rosenbaum touched off three days of rioting in Crown Heights. Authorities found many of the Hasidim unwilling to ignore the Rosenbaum murder. And so for three hot and sweltering days in New York City in 1991, many Jews of Crown Heights had simply decided they would not rely on the authorities to seek justice for Yankel Rosenbaum. And certainly, many African Americans in Crown Heights were willing to step around the law as well.

"At one point, I heard the distinctive pop of gunfire," wrote Larry Celona. "About a dozen cops ran around the corner and arrested the gunman, who was only probably shooting in the air. It only added to the

tension. Everyone was jittery. Then came a flurry of flying bottles, cans and rocks—like a sudden summer storm. Hecklers hurled debris from the back of a crowd straight at police. I stood just 10 feet from one riot-clad cop who was pelted with a bottle that shattered the plastic shield covering his face. Through the jagged plastic cracks, I saw a look of total panic. Fellow cops carried him away.

"Then a red Camaro loudly gunned its motor and headed straight toward a line of cops across the street from me. It hit a pole and stopped dead—and a dozen cops ran right over, pulling out the driver and handcuffing him. More cops were arriving all the time, but they were doing nothing but holding their ground."

While reporters and others look on, a police officer scuffles with a protester during the 1991 riots in Crown Heights. During the three-day disturbance, rabbinical student Yankel Rosenbaum lost his life in a stabbing.

■   ■   ■

The Reverend Al Sharpton soon found himself caught up in the tensions. On the morning after Gavin

Cato and Yankel Rosenbaum lost their lives, Sharpton was having breakfast in a Harlem restaurant with Alton Maddox when an assistant reached him, gave him a brief summation of what had happened the night before, and informed him that Gavin Cato's parents wanted to contact him. A few minutes later, Sharpton received a call from Gavin's father. "Reverend Sharpton, I'm the father of the young man killed and I would really like you to come out here," Carmel Cato said. "I believe there was some wrong here because the police roughed me up when I tried to get my son from under the car."

Sharpton headed for Crown Heights. He found an atmosphere thick with hatred. He met with the Cato family and accompanied them to the morgue to identify Gavin's body. On the way back from the morgue, Sharpton and the others found themselves in the path of rioting blacks and Jews.

Peter Noel, a reporter for the weekly newspaper The *Village Voice*, witnessed the rioting that day. Noel, a West Indies black, waded into the melee to save the life of Isaac Bitton, a Jew who had been cornered by a mob of blacks.

"I saved him," Noel said. "I'm not trying to be a hero for that. I was trying to just hold him and try to get him away from the crowd, and people were shouting . . . and, you know, sticks and stones were just coming from everywhere. I just saw another human being who was not a soldier in this combat. He was just a victim. Well, he was Jewish, yes, but he was a victim. He was not part of this combat that was happening at that point in time and I couldn't see him just go down like that. I was not a soldier in this war, either."

Sharpton returned to Crown Heights the next day. He was still helping the Cato family with funeral arrangements. Again, he found a riot. This time, young blacks gathered in front of a Hasidic synagogue. Soon, they were tossing bricks. The police arrived, broke up the riot and made dozens of arrests. Sharpton complained, though, that while the police

seemed to be doing a good job of picking up rioting blacks, few Jews had been taken into custody. Sharpton knew they were committing violence as well. Mayor Dinkins invited Sharpton to a meeting to explore ways to end the violence in Crown Heights. Sharpton insisted that the black rioters be released from jail. Dinkins feared their release could spark more violence, but he grudgingly agreed.

That weekend, Gavin Cato was buried. Three thousand people marched in the funeral procession.

"Though you could cut the tension in the air, it was the first nonviolent march of the week," Sharpton said. "A lot of the hard-core types were grumbling, 'We want to burn down Crown Heights,' but I said, 'Ya'll burned for three days and it didn't do nothing but get a

At an evening memorial service for Gavin Cato, Sharpton marches through Crown Heights with the young boy's father, Carmel Cato. Sharpton remained at the side of the Cato family after the fatal car accident that ended Gavin's life.

bunch of young kids locked up, who we had to get out. Now I'm going to show you how to do it.'"

■   ■   ■

Yosef Lifsh, who had been arrested following the accident, was released after a grand jury concluded he had not purposely or carelessly run over Gavin. Lifsh left court immediately for Kennedy Airport in New York, where he boarded a flight to Israel.

Sharpton urged the Cato family to file a lawsuit against Lifsh—to sue for monetary compensation for Gavin's death in civil court. The lawsuit was filed, but a judge ordered that the case could not be heard until Lifsh was served with an official copy.

So Sharpton, accompanied by Alton Maddox, caught a flight for Israel. They knew their chances of finding Lifsh in the Middle East country were slim, but under international law the suit could be delivered to the American embassy, which the courts in the United States would consider an acceptable delivery of the papers. After a 10-hour flight, Sharpton and Maddox arrived in the Israeli city of Tel Aviv, and took a taxi directly to the American embassy.

"We had a very nice meeting in the embassy," Sharpton said. "We served them [the legal papers], and they said they would serve Lifsh if they could find him. They gave us a receipt, then we had coffee and headed back to the airport."

Back in the United States, somebody had to answer for the murder of Yankel Rosenbaum. The police caught up with Lemrick Nelson, a 17-year-old Crown Heights African American, and charged him with stabbing the rabbinical student.

Nelson went to trial in late 1992. Most of the jurors were black. Prosecutors offered a bloody knife as evidence as well as testimony that Rosenbaum had identified Nelson as his attacker before he died. Nevertheless, Nelson was found not guilty. In a scene reminiscent of the Day of Outrage, which followed the verdicts in the Howard Beach case, angry people flooded into the streets to demonstrate their anger over the Nelson verdict. This time, though, the protesters weren't black; they were white. The Hasidic Jewish community of Crown Heights rose up in a violent outburst.

"No justice, no peace!" the Hasidim shouted as they marched through the streets of Crown Heights.

Soon after the verdict, a group of Hasidic Jews assaulted a homeless black man named Ralph Nimmons. Sharpton met with Nimmons and advised him to refuse to cooperate with investigators until a special prosecutor was appointed in his case, but this time the authorities flatly refused to be a part of the strategy Sharpton had used for Tawana Brawley and Cedric Sandiford. The Nimmons case soon lost the attention of the public.

But the Rosenbaum case did not. After Nelson's acquittal in a New York state court, Jewish leaders in the city called for a federal investigation of the murder. Sharpton joined in the demand for a federal probe.

"Justice is not something we oppose," he told a reporter. "I always ask the federal government to come in. They refused to come for Michael Griffith and Yusuf Hawkins. That doesn't mean they shouldn't come now. Certainly they should, but not to create a double standard. . . . We are against murder. The question is: Is everyone else against murder except when it comes to us? Let's play by one set of rules."

Lemrick Nelson came to trial in federal court in 1997. There is no murder charge in federal law—that is a charge that can be tried only in the state courts. But federal prosecutors charged Nelson with violating Rosenbaum's civil rights—they asserted that by taking Rosenbaum's life, Nelson had denied the man his rights as a U.S. citizen.

This time, Nelson was convicted. Also convicted

A year after the Crown Heights riots, Lemrick Nelson (right) was acquitted of the murder of Yankel Rosenbaum. In 1997, after Sharpton and Jewish leaders demanded a federal investigation, Nelson was eventually convicted of a separate charge of violating Rosenbaum's civil rights.

was Charles Price, 44, who also attacked Rosenbaum that night in 1991. Nelson was sentenced to 19 years in prison; Price got 22 years.

"What about my civil rights? You violated my civil rights," Nelson complained to prosecutors as he was led out of the courtroom.

Later, 91 Crown Heights Jews sued the city government, alleging that the police did not act quickly enough to protect them from rioters. The case was settled before it went to court when the city agreed to pay the plaintiffs $1.1 million. "I apologize to the citizens of Crown Heights, to the Rosenbaum family and to all of the people that were affected by this," said Mayor Rudolph Giuliani, who succeeded David Dinkins as mayor of New York City.

Dinkins reacted harshly to the settlement, insisting that the police—who were acting under his orders—responded properly to the riots and that Giuliani agreed to the settlement because he feared the political muscle of New York's Jewish community. "The mayor has thrown a tremendous amount of money at a baseless claim," Dinkins fumed.

In the aftermath of Crown Heights, Sharpton insisted that blacks and Jews continue to recognize a common bond between them: a long and arduous struggle against discrimination and prejudice. "The natural ties that have bound us in the past must be re-established," he said. "Jewish spokespersons must speak out more forcefully when black rights are trampled, just as blacks must protest every instance of anti-Semitism. Whether blacks and Jews on both sides realize it, our civil and human rights are intertwined. Those who paint swastikas on synagogues are inclined to be white supremacists as well. Gangs who get their kicks from beating up a black person in 'their' neighborhood are likely to keep Jews out as well."

■   ■   ■

Peter Noel and Isaac Bitton met again in 1993, seeing each other for the first time since the night in 1991 when Noel pulled Bitton from the clutches of a mob. A documentary movie crew was on hand to film the reunion.

"What's up man? Long time, no see," Noel said.

"Long time no see," answered Bitton. "You didn't call me back when I called you."

"I spent four days in Israel," Noel said. "You know, it was kind of crazy, man."

"You liked it?" Bitton asked.

"It was real nice," Noel said.

"This guy," Bitton noted, gratefully gesturing to his rescuer. "I just can say he was sent by heaven, that's all. Right time. Right place."

8

"I CAN FLY!"

⚘

ᴀʟ SHARPTON STRODE to the center of the stage in the ballroom of the Rihga Royal Hotel in midtown Manhattan and faced hundreds of his supporters, who were laughing, screaming, and chanting his name: "Sharpton! Sharpton! Sharpton!"

It was the night of September 9, 1997. Hours before, the polls had closed in New York City, ending a spirited Democratic Party primary campaign in the race for mayor. Three candidates had spent months on the campaign trail, rising early in the morning to greet voters at subway stations, knocking on doors in Brooklyn neighborhoods, shaking hands at Little League games in Queens, and then speaking in the evening at fund-raising dinners, debates, and community meetings.

One of those candidates was Ruth W. Messinger, the Manhattan Borough president. A veteran political leader in New York, Messinger had lined up support from many elected officials, as well as from other traditional Democratic power bases such as the unions and the city's wealthy liberal residents. From the start, she had been considered the favorite in the race.

Another candidate was Sal Albanese, a city councilman. He was a former school teacher who promised to overhaul the city's troubled schools. Albanese was a veteran New York political organizer, and he was sure to draw votes from the city's closely-knit neighborhoods.

The 1990s saw Sharpton as a committed politician with an ever-growing constituency. Here, he proudly announces his decision to seek the Democratic nomination for New York City mayor.

Sharpton was the third candidate. The press and political pundits thought that he was the least likely to win. They had criticized him for his rabble-rousing and sermonizing and noted that although he had twice run for the U.S. Senate, he never came close to winning.

But as he prepared to speak to the throng of supporters at the Rihga Royal Hotel, there was clearly magic in the air. Unofficial results from the city's polling places showed that although Sharpton had not won the Democratic primary, he had beaten Albanese and denied Messinger the 40 percent of the vote she needed to move on to the general election to face the city's incumbent mayor, Republican Rudolph Giuliani. Now, it appeared Messinger would have to face Sharpton in a runoff election to pick the party's nominee.

"I told you I would be at the gate before you pick me up on the radar screen," Sharpton told his supporters, as they shouted "Amen!" and "You got that!"

The reverend waited for the applause to die down. By his side stood his wife Kathy and daughters Ashley and Dominique. Sharpton was thinner than he had been in years, having lost weight through diet and exercise. His hair was still straight in the James Brown style, but now his temples were flecked with gray. He raised his hands to speak again.

First Sharpton told the crowd that he was prepared to beat Messinger in the runoff and face Giuliani in November. He added, "The real loser is Giuliani. He will not be able to ignore the issues and the constituency that I've tried to represent. Those days are over. The issues of unemployment and police brutality and schools not working are on the front burner. You can run, Rudy, but you can't hide."

■　　■　　■

In early 1992, Sharpton had found himself at a crossroads in his life. Following the stabbing at the

Bensonhurst rally, he had reevaluated his mission and decided that if he wished to improve conditions for African Americans, he had to widen his appeal and alter his message. Sharpton decided to use the political arena to achieve these goals. His first opportunity had come in the early fall of 1992, in the Democratic primary for U.S. Senate. He said:

> As I thought it through, I realized that I might be able to do statewide in New York what Jesse Jackson did nationally in 1984 and 1988, which is enter Democratic primaries and put our black community issues and problems on the table, voice our feelings, state our concerns. . . . I also thought I would be able to mobilize grassroots activity and help get out new voters who could participate in electing new blood in some of the local races. With all the noise about U.S. president and Senate, it's easy to overlook congressional races, state senate and state assembly. You've also got things like city councils and boards of education. Finally, there were no blacks in the U.S. Senate at the time, and there had never been a black elected statewide in New York at the time. So I had plenty of reasons to go for it.

Sharpton knew he could find a large African-American constituency among Democrats. Throughout U.S. history, the Democratic Party's influence has grown with the expansion of American cities. When blacks headed north following the Civil War and Reconstruction, they settled in the cities and joined the Democratic Party, which since the 1800s had increased its numbers by inviting African Americans, as well as European immigrants, into its ranks. Although there have been black leaders in the Republican Party, including U.S. Representative J.C. Watts Jr. and Secretary of State Colin Powell, most blacks are members of the Democratic Party. For the most part, the Democratic Party continues to maintain much of its support in the cities. New York, for example, has five times as many Democrats as Republicans.

But that doesn't automatically mean all cities elect only Democrats. When a party's elected members fail to deal with such problems as high crime, poor schools, crumbling roads, and corruption, city voters—like voters everywhere—will replace them, regardless of which party they represent.

Sharpton found an old foe in the 1992 Democratic primary for U.S. Senate—State Attorney General Robert Abrams. Two other candidates in the race were Elizabeth Holtzman, the city comptroller of New York, and Geraldine Ferraro, a former member of Congress from New York who had run for vice president in 1984.

Sharpton was given little chance to win the primary for the right to face Republican incumbent Alfonse D'Amato. The four candidates met for several debates in the weeks leading up to the primary, and it was clear that Ferraro and Holtzman regarded Abrams as the front-runner, and took dead aim at chipping away his lead. Sharpton decided to stay out of the fray.

"I took my chance to run for office too seriously to smear it with that kind of behavior," Sharpton said. "I was always thinking about and took to heart all the bloodshed and death that it took to get black voters the right to vote. I couldn't think of all those sacrifices and feel I could make a mockery of them by engaging in sleaze."

Instead, he talked about issues he felt the voters wanted to hear. He called for the appointment of a permanent special prosecutor in cases involving police brutality and racial violence. Also, Sharpton opposed tax breaks for corporations. Politicians had for years advocated cutting taxes for big companies to induce them to create jobs, but most ordinary taxpayers had come to regard such tax incentives as

As a Democratic candidate for the New York senate seat, Sharpton participates in a 1992 television debate; from the right are Liz Holtzman, Geraldine Ferraro, and Sharpton's old legal adversary, Robert Abrams.

what many call "corporate welfare." Later, other political leaders would realize such tax breaks were not popular among the voters, and they adopted similar positions.

But while Sharpton had confidence in his issues and he staked out the high ground in the bitter campaign, he still had many hurdles to overcome. For example, the other candidates were raising and spending millions of dollars in the race. Sharpton's campaign war chest would amount to a paltry $63,000. After the election, he said:

"We just got up every day that fall and did our best, just kept trying, kept hammering those issues, kept on going. . . . As it got down to the wire, the press said the best I would do was 5 percent. The night of the election I sat in my office on Bedford Avenue, listening to the returns. There was a lot on

After finishing third in the U.S. Senate primary, Sharpton makes a speech to his supporters. Joining him at his side are his wife, Kathy, and his daughters Ashley (left) and Dominique (right).

my mind, all the places I had been, the people I had known. It felt like it was coming down to this one night. I had put my career on the line. If, after presenting and pleading my case all fall, I came back with less than a majority of the black vote, everyone would say that it proved I was a loudmouth and a bully, that I had no following, no constituency. I would be invalidated."

Sharpton did not win the primary, but with 166,000 votes, there was no question that he had been a legitimate candidate and could be considered a strong force in New York State politics. He finished in front of Holtzman, carrying 67 percent of the black vote and 14 percent of the total vote. Governor Mario Cuomo, who had been a target of Sharpton's bitter attacks over his stewardship of the

Crown Heights and Bensonhurst investigations, admitted that he was impressed with Sharpton's showing in the race. Said Cuomo: "The real winner tonight is Al Sharpton."

■   ■   ■

Two years after the 1992 U.S. Senate primary, Sharpton was again a candidate. Again, he chose to run for the Democratic nomination for U.S. Senate, this time against incumbent Daniel Patrick Moynihan. A Democrat, Moynihan had long been one of New York's most popular political figures, as well as one of the nation's leading experts on the federal budget. But Sharpton believed that Moynihan had lost touch with New York City's people, particularly the black neighborhoods, and he thought the veteran senator might be vulnerable.

Sharpton said:

> I started my campaign at the corner of Franklin Avenue and Fulton Street in Brooklyn, under the falling-down Franklin Avenue El tracks, to illustrate how the infrastructure of urban areas had been allowed to deteriorate in the home state of the chairman of the Senate Finance Committee. Moynihan had all this juice in Washington, but public transportation was collapsing in Bedford-Stuyvesant. We stood out there in the rain with about 500 people, and I talked about how I had ridden over that day on the same train on the same tracks as I had once ridden with my mother, and how far I had come while at the same time the city had fallen so far. Did Daniel Patrick Moynihan understand what was happening? Did he care?

Sharpton failed to beat Moynihan, but his showing in the primary was again impressive. This time, he received 187,000 votes—slightly more votes than he had received in 1992, but his share of the total vote was much higher. That year saw a poorer voter turnout than in 1992.

"That was a real achievement against someone the stature of Daniel Patrick Moynihan," Sharpton said. "I received a much higher percentage of the black vote than in 1992—87 percent against 67 percent, even running against an incumbent who spent $4 million in mailings and television in the primary versus my $100,000."

Sharpton would soon find himself involved in other political fights, but not as a candidate. Indeed, some of the nation's most important political leaders now saw the need to ask Al Sharpton for his help in their campaigns.

In 2000, presidential candidate Al Gore campaigned in New York City and met with Sharpton, hoping to enlist his aid in the race for the White House. "We made it clear we're going to meet with Democratic leaders across New York, including representatives of important communities," said Gore campaign spokesman Chris Lehane, when reporters pressed him for details on the Gore-Sharpton meeting.

Another political figure who courted Sharpton was Hillary Rodham Clinton, the Democratic candidate for U.S. Senate in New York State. In 2000, Moynihan decided to retire and Mrs. Clinton, the first lady, had been invited to run for the open seat by New York Democratic leaders. "Hillary Clinton is reaching out to as many New Yorkers as possible and I'm sure that will include the Reverend Sharpton," said Clinton campaign spokesman Howard Rolfson. "We are not taking any vote for granted."

Hillary Rodham Clinton went on to win her election, but Gore lost to Republican George W. Bush. For a month following Election Day, the Gore-Bush outcome remained in doubt due to an incomplete vote count in Florida. Soon questions of voting irregularities arose. Among the areas where the counting was challenged were the black precincts in Florida cities.

Sharpton and other African-American leaders headed to Florida to call for full recounts. Sharpton filed a lawsuit in the U.S. District Court in Florida, alleging that Bush "engaged in a series of acts, and refrained from engaging in other acts, that led the Black American, African American, Hispanic American, among other minority groups, to be excluded from participating in, or having their vote totals included in the final certification." The lawsuit accused Bush and other Republican leaders of violating the 1965 Voting Rights Act, a law adopted during the civil rights movement that guaranteed blacks access to the polls.

Among the charges raised by black leaders following the election were that poll workers in the black precincts were improperly trained and unable to provide voters with the proper instructions for filling out their ballots, and that the state government in Florida failed to provide Haitian-American voters, who speak primarily French, with bilingual ballots.

"We had reports of checkpoints being set up by police in some predominantly black neighborhoods," said Jean Ross, a spokeswoman for the NAACP. "People were pulled over and detained. I would call that intimidation."

The courts soon threw out the Sharpton suit as well as other legal challenges filed against the outcome of the 2000 presidential election. Although many opponents shared Sharpton's disapproval of the outcome, George W. Bush took office as the nation's 43rd president.

Still, after the election, Sharpton remained critical of the new Bush administration. He was among black leaders who disputed Bush's selection of New Jersey governor Christine Todd Whitman to head the U.S. Environmental Protection Agency—the federal division that enforces laws protecting rivers, forests, and other natural resources.

Many Americans disputed Republican George W. Bush's election victory in 2000, challenging the final vote count for the state of Florida. Sharpton and others protested against what they thought were biased voting procedures in the black precincts of the state.

For years, Whitman had been criticized for her administration's handling of "racial profiling" charges that were being made against the New Jersey State Police. Sharpton noted that although state troopers had been accused for years of routinely stopping black motorists without cause on the highways, a complete investigation into the charges of racial profiling was never made.

Sharpton argued that as EPA administrator Whitman would turn a blind eye to the environmental hazards threatening minority communities. "How can we trust her judgment in where to put toxic waste dumps?" Sharpton asked. "How can she deal with subtle, institutional racism when it took her three years to find blatant racism on the highways that she travels everyday?"

Whitman was eventually confirmed for the position,

taking office despite the questions on her record of dealing fairly with minorities.

■   ■   ■

By participating in the campaigns of Al Gore and Hillary Rodham Clinton or in the protests against George W. Bush and Christine Todd Whitman, Sharpton demonstrated that he was now a figure of national political prominence. His achievements in the 1997 New York City mayoral primary had also helped boost him into that role.

At that stage political power in New York had shifted away from the Democrats. Republican Rudolph Giuliani had won the mayoral seat in 1993 from David Dinkins, who had been unable to stem the decay of New York's neighborhoods or ensure New Yorkers that the streets were free of violent criminals. Rudolph Giuliani had ousted Dinkins in the 1993 race by promising to give police a free hand to stamp out crime.

Many black leaders, including Sharpton, believed the New York City police had gone too far in this mandate to eliminate crime. Activists complained of the police station beating of Jamaican immigrant Abner Louima, as well as the death of Amadou Diallo, a West African who had been shot by police. As the 1997 campaign unfolded, polls showed that New York City's black community desperately wanted Giuliani out of Gracie Mansion—the city's official residence for the mayor.

After the death of Mother Teresa, the internationally revered humanitarian, Sharpton had some timely words for his supporters: "I felt that Mother Teresa stood for the underdog. She reminded the world about our commitment to the poor. I think it is appropriate that all New Yorkers pause and remember her and exalt her because it is that type of spirit for the underdog and the poor that we must make contagious."

There would be no runoff against Messinger.

Sharpton delivers another impassioned speech in front of the Lincoln Memorial, where thousands gathered for the "Redeem the Dream" march, commemorating the 37th anniversary of Martin Luther King Jr.'s "I Have a Dream" speech.

Although the election night total showed that Sharpton had denied his opponent the 40 percent of the vote she needed to move on to the general election, the official count—conducted days later—enabled her to gain more votes, mostly from the absentee ballots that had been cast weeks before the election but had arrived late. The final vote showed Messinger with 165,383—40.16 percent of the votes cast in the New York Democratic mayoral primary. Sharpton garnered 131,888, followed by Albanese, who received 86,619. Later, Messinger would lose the general election to Giuliani.

But on that incandescent night in the ballroom of the Rihga Royal Hotel, the Reverend Al Sharpton told his supporters that they were standing at the threshold of a new era in New York politics.

"I got wings and I can fly," he said. "We are going to fly from the outhouse to Gracie Mansion. We're going to fly. This is our date. This is our time. I can fly! I can fly! I can fly!"

CHRONOLOGY

———— ❦ ————

1954	Alfred Charles Sharpton Jr. is born on October 3, in Brooklyn, New York
1959	At age 4, preaches first sermon at Washington Temple Church of God in Christ in Brooklyn
1964	Is ordained a minister by Bishop Frederick Douglass Washington
1968	Martin Luther King Jr. is assassinated in Memphis, Tennessee, on April 4
1969	Sharpton is appointed youth director of Operation Breadbasket, the Southern Christian Leadership Conference's program to boycott businesses using unfair employment methods
1971	Organizes National Youth Movement, an association of young people dedicated to activism
1972	Works in the campaign of Shirley Chisholm, a black congresswoman from New York City who runs for president
1973	Promotes shows for James Brown, the "Godfather of Soul"
1984	Helps promote the Jacksons' Victory Tour
1986	Organizes protests in Howard Beach, Queens, after Michael Griffith is struck and killed by a car while fleeing a mob of white attackers
1987	On February 9, four men are charged with murder and manslaughter in the Griffith case; in Wappingers Falls, New York, Tawana Brawley claims to have been abducted and raped by six white men; Sharpton and a legal team offer their assistance
1988	New York periodical *Newsday* publishes a series of stories identifying Sharpton as an FBI informant; the Brawley grand jury ends its investigation, concluding that the accuser had not been assaulted; Abrams launches investigations into the activities of Sharpton, Maddox, and Mason
1989	On August 23, Yusuf Hawkins is fatally stabbed by a white mob in Bensonhurst, Brooklyn
1991	On January 12, Sharpton is stabbed by a white assailant while preparing to lead a protest march through Bensonhurst, Brooklyn; rioting breaks out in Crown Heights, Brooklyn, following the deaths of Gavin Cato and Yankel Rosenbaum

1992	Sharpton asks Judge Francis X. Egitto to show leniency to Michael Riccardi, the man who stabbed him at the Bensonhurst protest; Lemrick Nelson is acquitted of Rosenbaum's murder in state court; Sharpton runs for U.S. Senate, garnering 166,000 votes to finish third in the Democratic primary
1994	Sharpton receives 187,000 votes in the U.S. Senate primary in New York State
1997	Lemrick Nelson and Charles Price are convicted in federal court for violating Rosenbaum's civil rights; Sharpton finishes second in New York City Democratic mayoral primary behind Ruth Messinger
1998	Steven Pagones, an assistant district attorney under suspicion in the Brawley case, wins a $66,000 judgment in a lawsuit filed against Sharpton
2000	Sharpton helps the campaigns of presidential candidate Al Gore and U.S. Senate candidate Hillary Rodham Clinton
2001	Sharpton opposes the selection of New Jersey governor Christine Todd Whitman as head of the U.S. Environmental Protection Agency

BIBLIOGRAPHY

Books and Periodicals

Arnett, Elsa C. "Struggles Unite Blacks and Jews, but Economic Forces Divide." *Seattle Times*, August 12, 2000.

Diamond, Edwin. "The Sound Bites and the Fury." *New York*, March 28, 1988.

Duke, Lynne. "The Mainstreaming of Al Sharpton." *Washington Post*, March 7, 2000.

Fried, Joseph P. "Three in Howard Beach Attack are Guilty of Manslaughter." *The New York Times*, December 22, 1987.

Klein, Michael. *The Man Behind the Sound Bite: The Real Story of Al Sharpton*. New York: Castillo International, 1991.

Kunen, James S. "Trials of Tawana." *People Weekly*, July 4, 1988.

Manegold, Catherine S. "The Reformation of a Street Preacher." *The New York Times Sunday Magazine*, January 24, 1993.

Noel, Peter. "Father of the Movement." *The Village Voice*, March 31, 1999.

Rennert, Richard. *Civil Rights Leaders*. New York: Chelsea House, 1993.

Richardson, Ben, and William A. Fahey. *Great Black Americans*. New York: Thomas Y. Crowell Co., 1976.

Sharpton, Al, and Anthony Walton. *Go and Tell Pharaoh: The Autobiography of Al Sharpton*. New York: Doubleday, 1996.

Sleeper, Jim. "A Man of Too Many Parts." *The New Yorker*, January 25, 1993.

Tomasky, Michael. "Four Candidates and a Funeral." *New York*, May 12, 1997.

Vedantam, Shakar, and Richard Lezin Jones. "NAACP to Sue, Alleging Violations at Florida Polls." *Philadelphia Inquirer*, November 30, 2000.

Websites

ABC News

"Sharpton's New World: Hillary Clinton's Campaign Comes Courting." *http://www.abcnews.go.com/sections/politics/DailyNews/sharpton991102.html*

"The Montgomery Bus Boycott."
http://www.watson.org/~lisa/blackhistory/civilrights-55-65/montbus.html

"From Small Beginnings: the Montgomery Bus Boycott."
http://facstaff.uww.edu/mohamp/ethnic9d.html

"Brown v. Board of Education Issue: Racial Segregation in Public Schools."
http://www.pbs.org/jefferson/enlight/brown.htm

"A Brief History of Civil Rights in the United States of America."
http://www.coloradocollege.edu/Dept/PS/faculty/loevy/civil%20rights.html

Salon Magazine

"The Salon Interview: Al Sharpton."
http://www.salonmag.com/weekly/sharpton1.html

INDEX

PICTURE CREDITS

HAL MARCOVITZ is a journalist for *The Morning Call*, a newspaper based in Allentown, Pennsylvania. He has written more than 20 books for young readers. He lives in Chalfont, Pennsylvania, with his wife, Gail, and daughters, Ashley and Michelle.

NATHAN IRVIN HUGGINS, one of America's leading scholars in the field of black studies, helped select the titles for the BLACK AMERICANS OF ACHIEVEMENT series, for which he also served as senior consulting editor. He was the W. E. B. DuBois Professor of History and Afro-American Studies at Harvard University and the director of the W. E. B. DuBois Institute for Afro-American Research at Harvard. He received his doctorate from Harvard in 1962 and returned there as professor in 1980 after teaching at Columbia University, the University of Massachusetts, Lake Forest College, and the California State University, Long Beach. He was the author of four books and dozens of articles, including *Black Odyssey: The Afro-American Ordeal in Slavery*, *The Harlem Renaissance*, and *Slave and Citizen: The Life of Frederick Douglass*, and was associated with the Children's Television Workshop, National Public Radio, the Boston Athenaeum, the Museum of Afro-American History, the Howard Thurman Educational Trust, and Upward Bound. Professor Huggins died in 1989, at the age of 62, in Cambridge, Massachusetts.